European Working Class

A Short History
of the
European Working Class

Wolfgang Abendroth

Monthly Review Press
New York and London

Originally published as
Sozialgeschichte der europäischen Arbeiterbewegung
by Suhrkamp Verlag, Frankfurt/Main, Germany,
copyright © 1965 by Suhrkamp Verlag

Translated by Nicholas Jacobs and Brian Trench
Postscript translated by Joris de Bres

Library of Congress Catalog Card Number: 72-81766

First Modern Reader Paperback Edition 1973
Second Printing

Monthly Review Press
62 West 14th Street, New York, N.Y. 10011
21 Theobalds Road, London WC1X 8SL

Manufactured in the United States of America

Foreword

Ever since the English Revolution of the seventeenth century and the American and French Revolutions of the eighteenth, the originally bourgeois movement for liberty and justice has changed the world. The concept of freedom has become a fundamental principle of all political organizations and ideologies, even where it was once denounced by governments and by feudal and absolutist political theorists as utopian and criminal nonsense. The working class transformed this call for liberty from being a political slogan and made it a social demand. Ever since the Industrial Revolution, this demand has been made not only on behalf of the white race but of all mankind, including that great majority which the colonial expansion of industrial capitalism had initially subjected to exploitation and oppression.

There have been times when the activity of the working-class movement has differed widely from its original claims, and it has not yet attained its goal. In the United States and in West Europe it has achieved a material standard of living which only fifty years ago ruling class theorists would have regarded as a dangerous dream threatening civilization with idleness and sensuality. In East Europe it has transformed the structure of society but undergone a period of despotism, just as after 1789 the bourgeois revolution in France appeared to end in the Napoleonic Empire, although it had swept away the basis of feudalism.

In capitalist countries where the working class has the highest material living standards – in the United States and in West Europe – the labour movement appears to be paralysed within the self-imposed limitations of trade union conformism and to have adopted the ideology of the ruling class. In exactly the same way, after the foundation of the Reich in 1871 the German bourgeoisie welcomed the Hohenzollerns, idolized Bismarck, and turned its back on the struggle for parliamentary democracy – all for the sake of economic prosperity. Was this, and is not its modern counterpart, not just a passing, if significant, phase of historical development? And would it not be unpardonable provincialism to assume that the present situation in West Europe or anywhere else constitutes the final outcome and end of world history?

Only a study of the development of the working-class movement in its historical totality can help us in the search for a full answer to this question – an answer on which all our efforts to gain a clear understanding of our present world depends. The working class movement began as a product of European history. It is therefore logical to start by limiting our study to Europe, although it should not be forgotten that the revolutions beyond its confines are now putting into practice ideas which have their origins in the European working-class movement.

It is the aim of this book to further such study, and its form and content are determined and limited by this aim. I have intentionally omitted all scholarly apparatus because my purpose was to write a readable analysis and not a text-book. That does not mean that I have not made use of the relevant literature. But I do not want to give the impression that this book is more than a short outline. It is not the comprehensive history of the European working-class movement which, despite many preliminary studies – above all Julius Braunthal's *History of the International* – has still to be written.

Wolfgang Abendroth
1965

Author's note: The original edition of this book was written seven years ago. For this English-language edition I have added a postscript on the recent history of working-class parties and trade unions in Europe.

1971

The Beginnings up to
the Defeat of 1848

From the mid sixteenth to the last third of the eighteenth century, the characteristic form of capitalist production was manufacture. In its first phase, artisans of different trades worked in one workshop with unskilled labourers under the control of a single capitalist. Later, manufacture developed into a form of collaboration between artisans of the same trade whose previous work was divided into different operations and separated. Each worker's contribution to production as a whole was thus reduced to a series of mechanical actions and production costs could be lowered. Both these forms of manufacture destroyed the professional pride and future hopes of the apprentice. Objectively, in the era before manufacture, the workers also depended on selling their labour-power but they still had a real chance of eventually becoming independent. As long as the laws of the guilds limited this independence, it was the declared aim of the apprentice clubs, besides securing better work and living conditions, to go beyond these limits. In exceptional circumstances, their demands sometimes went still further. They were however unable to generate a movement with any continuity.

The further evolution of manufacture changed this, even when the work of dependent producers was not concentrated under one roof but took the form of home industry. With the introduction of manufacture, work lost the tangible, meaningful unity it had still retained for the master craftsman's apprentice. The social division of labour led to the subordination of the individual who became a completely isolated component, cut off from any sense of the meaning of the process as a whole and subjected to rigorous discipline. The industrial revolution in the last third of the eighteenth century only carried this process to its logical conclusion.

The origin and centre of this continuously expanding revolution was the machine. The worker capable of handling a single tool was superseded by a mechanism capable of operating a number of similar tools simultaneously. The human organ was superseded by mechanical organization, independent of the limitations of human power. This totally transformed the whole productive process. Whereas in manufacture the organization of social labour was purely subjective – a combination of different operations – the new modern industry had in machinery a purely objective productive organism which converted the labourer into a mere appendage of an already existing material condition of production. Henceforth it was no longer necessary to have either particular physical strength or hard-won practical skill to do most of the work. This brought with it a drastic increase in female and child labour, with disastrous consequences for the physical and mental well-being of the population; consequences which characterized the first decade of nineteenth-century European capitalism and were repeated in the twentieth-century industrialization of the former colonies and of 'developing countries' with capitalist property relations.

Capitalists are forced to seek maximum profits, so in its first phase industrialization automatically led to the continuous utilization of machinery. Thus, the triumph of the machine led to the lengthening of the working day and the intensification of labour. In the early period of manufacture, despite differences of interest between various social groups, the workers tolerated the system. This was particularly true of peasants, deprived of their existence on the land by the systematic enclosures carried out by powerful landlords, and for whom the new industries provided an alternative livelihood. Nevertheless, this period also saw conflicts over wages and working hours and it was these conflicts that gave the workers their first taste of the differences of social interest between themselves and their employers. Now, with the coming of industrialization, the machines themselves competed with workers as means of production, throwing them out of work and creating an industrial reserve army wherever they were introduced. It was possible for such workers to find employment elsewhere, but under worse conditions. As Ricardo said: 'The same factor which can increase income from the land (for landowners and capitalists) can simultaneously create a population surplus and make conditions for the labourers worse.'

Thus it was hardly surprising that the workers' first reaction was to destroy the machines. Seventeenth-century Europe had already seen revolts against the first ribbon and lace looms. At first the machines had been forbidden. The Elector of Saxony only allowed them in 1765. The first mechanical wool-shearing machines were destroyed by English workers in 1758. To control the continuing mass panic, Parliament passed a law threatening anybody found guilty of destroying factories or machine-breaking with execution. The workers in turn repeatedly petitioned Parliament for the outlawing of machines. At the beginning of the nineteenth century they again resorted to more violent mass action. From 1811 onwards the movement grew so strong that, despite Byron's outspoken appeal against such a law in the House of Lords in 1812, the government repeatedly fell back on legislation which made machine-breaking a capital offence.

The illusory, if understandable, resistance by the workers was thus finally broken by terror. It flickered into life once again after the execution of eighteen workers from York in 1813, but without substantial results. Gradually the English workers learnt, in Marx's words, 'to distinguish between the machinery and its employment by capital, and to direct their attacks not against the material instruments of production, but against the mode in which they are used'. However, machine-breaking lingered on into the second half of the nineteenth century and appeared in other countries at a corresponding level of industrialization – for example, the uprisings of the Lyons silk workers in 1831 and of the Silesian weavers in 1844.

The educational level of the workers in this first phase of industrialism was low and they were humiliated by being forced to sell not only their own labour-power but also that of their children at a steadily declining price in order to survive. The fact that the workers had to send their children into the factories instead of to school perpetuated their educational impoverishment. It was therefore not surprising that their reaction was violent. Already by the end of the Middle Ages, legislation combined with liberal ideologies based on a static concept of natural law had deprived the workers of the right to determine their own work and life by united action. In 1731 the Imperial Order of the Guilds, following virtually every European state, placed a common law ban on apprentice unions throughout the Holy Roman Empire. The bourgeois revolutions did nothing to change this. The rationalist protagonists of medieval natural law, the Physiocrats, and the classic liberal economists agreed that freedom and equality were best secured by guaranteeing the property relations of, and private competition between, numerous small producers, thus prohibiting the association of 'particular interest groups' whose power, they assumed, would only limit the freedom of others. As long as the workers continued to regard themselves as inferior 'plebeians', they also remained the prisoners of such ideas. So the most intelligent, who saw that they could only regain their own rights by demanding equal political rights for all and thus prevent the state being abused in the interests of a minority, and who made all the appropriate claims for all the liberties embodied in natural law, still did not distinguish their demands from those of the radical bourgeois democrats. Thus, it was the working class which, besides the revolutionary intelligentsia, was the chief defendant of the French Revolution outside France, and it was the English apprentices and workers who provided the social basis for the ideology of international solidarity in the struggle for democracy and human rights, in defence of the Revolution against the European coalition. At a time when Thomas Paine was explaining democratic natural law in *The Rights of Man* (published early in the 1790s), British workers and artisans were organizing themselves in Corresponding Societies, the first of which was founded by Thomas Hardy, a London shoemaker, in 1792. Within two years, ten thousand British workers were members of such Societies, some of which gained sympathy in certain intellectual circles and among sections of the industrial bourgeoisie, particularly when the French wars cut Britain off from the continental market.

In October 1795 demonstrations broke out in London against George III and the Prime Minister, Pitt, demanding the end of the war against France. Agitation continued until the Mutiny of the Fleet in 1797 and was put down shortly after by the ban on Debating Clubs in 1799 and the passing, in the same year and in 1800, of

Combination Acts (supplemented by the suspension of Habeas Corpus in 1794) annulling the right to form trade unions. In Germany too, the Silesian weavers' uprising between 1792 and 1794 testified to the plebeian character of Jacobinism.

The French Revolution had paved the way for the recognition of human rights and the realization of the democratic ideal in Europe. This was mainly the achievement of the democratic franchise of the Constitution of 1793 and the revolutionary dictatorship of the Jacobins. Initially, however, this meant neither social nor economic independence for the working class under petty-bourgeois democracy. The European industrial boom, the impact on manufacture of the new application of machinery, only began under the protection of the continental blockade during the Revolutionary wars and the First Empire. Although apprentices and manufacturing workers were in the vanguard of the revolutionary struggle from 14 July 1789 to the fall of Robespierre on 9 Thermidor 1794, they were – even during the rule of the Committee of Public Safety – unable to obtain the repeal of the Girondin decree of 14 June 1791 which banned all workers' and artisans' associations on the grounds that they were a threat to liberty and the Declaration of the Rights of Man (given a purely individualist character by the Girondins). Thermidor and the substitution of the rule of the revolutionary intelligentsia and petty-bourgeoisie by that of the bourgeoisie proper ended the period of political action by the workers. Babeuf tried to exploit the situation of the Directory in 1796 by means of propaganda and the clandestine Conspiracy of Equals. He maintained that democracy had failed because of the contradiction between the proclamation of political equality and the absence of social equality, and he sought to establish a revolutionary dictatorship with the aim of building a socialist and agrarian society abolishing the right of inheritance. The trial of the conspirators and the execution of Babeuf sealed the fate of the movement, although Buonarroti's history of the Conspiracy, published in 1828, was of deep theoretical importance for the underground organizations of revolutionary democrats and workers during the July Monarchy, and its influence extended beyond France.

Thus the French Revolution succeeded in establishing important premisses for the future development of the European working class: an awareness of the necessity for both political democracy and international solidarity in the struggle for human rights. The experience of social conflict against the bourgeoisie had led to serious consideration of how society could be transformed, and this had its effect on small groups of workers in both Britain and France. For such people capitalist ownership of the means of production was now no longer an unquestioned or sacrosanct principle of economic life.

Although the period of the Directory, the Consulate and the First Empire crippled the French and continental working classes, exhausted as they were by revolutionary upheavals, industrialism spread swiftly through France and Western Germany where the bourgeoisie was in the ascendant. Its development was particularly intense during the military rule of Napoleon. The resulting increase in the bourgeoisie's economic power and the added importance of the industrial worker in relation to other workers were not at first especially pronounced. Nevertheless, despite the triumph of the Restoration, the new situation could not fail to have political consequences as soon as authority began to weaken. The anachronistic attitudes of the French Bourbons who simply ignored the real significance of the new classes, despite the impossibility of a return to the pre-Revolutionary order, forced the bourgeoisie to form a liberal opposition – an opposition which needed the workers as its fighting auxiliaries. It was within this opposition that the consciousness of the workers continued to develop.

This situation was even further advanced in England where industry had made even greater strides. Conservative reaction, reinforced by its victory over France, competed with the industrial bourgeoisie for political power, and this struggle had a much more positive outlook for democracy in England than elsewhere because of the much stronger position and greater self-confidence of the English bourgeoisie. As a result, England soon saw the resumption of the struggle for electoral reform, borne both by the industrial bourgeoisie which wanted to have its say in politics and to adjust the country's tariff and foreign policies to its own requirements, and by the new working class. In the mass demonstration of Peterloo in 1819 the workers first added their own social and political demands, marking a new phase in their struggle.

Contradictions within the ruling political and economic groups led to the repeal of the Combination Acts in 1824. The already existing but hitherto illegal trade unions could now fight in the open. In this period of economic boom, followed by a serious crisis after a year of speculation in 1825, the ruling classes hardly regarded the right to form unions as a dangerous concession. It was, however, partially withdrawn after a wave of strikes in 1825. But the English workers could no longer be deprived of the right to combine as such. Moreover the 1825 crisis had shown for the first time that, as soon as they had properly functioning unions, the workers were at least capable of successfully defending improvements in their living standards won in the preceding period of prosperity. The theories of Robert Owen and William King, founder of *The Co-operator*, helped the movement to establish stability. Socially it could depend on the skilled, and therefore better paid and better educated, workers required by the new era of industrialization. The conflict between the bourgeoisie and the landowners over electoral reform enabled the cooperative and trade union movements to develop and prepare for the day when their legal organizations could finally join the struggle for political democracy and the transformation of society in the spirit of cooperative socialism. By the time John Docherty organized the Grand Union of Spinners in 1829, and the National Association for the Protection of Labour was established in 1830, Owenism – hitherto philanthropic and reformist – had become one of the chief theoretical pillars of the working-class movement. Needless to say, the workers were completely cheated of their political rights by a new upper-class compromise in the form of the 1832 Reform Bill. However, for the time being, it was natural that the workers initially concentrated all their hopes in the trade unions and the cooperatives, especially as they had not yet suffered a decisive setback at this level.

In his *Report to the County of Lanark* (1820), Owen developed his plan for a 'labour market' which aimed to make it possible to exchange goods equivalent to the value of hours worked in the cooperatives. He intended this new economic order to compete alongside existing capitalism and gradually to replace it. In 1833 a plan was set up for the establishment of a General Labour Union.

The aim was to deprive capitalists of labour-power by collecting the workers into productive cooperatives and thus establish a socialist economy. In 1834 the Grand National Consolidated Trades Union was founded. Owen never thought in terms of class struggle and believed he could win over capitalist entrepreneurs to his cooperative scheme as well. Like Saint-Simon, he believed in the common interest of all the productive and industrial classes against those of the landlords and the state. His 'New Moral World' was supposed to evolve in perfect class harmony. In reality, however, increasing trade union activity led to more and more struggles for better work and living conditions for the workers and to vigorous counter-measures by the entrepreneurs. This led to the collapse of the giant union and its cooperative ideology. The factory owners refused to employ union members so the unions were forced to ask members to keep membership a secret. This gave the state a chance to attack them as secret organizations. The Grand National Union was taken unawares and went into quick decline. Only small skilled workers' unions remained. The many unskilled, and the lowest paid, workers simply dispersed. Owen's influence on the English working-class movement was extinguished, though his followers reappear periodically later, most significantly in 1844 at the foundation of the Rochdale Pioneers' Society, the forerunner of the consumers' cooperatives of our own day.

Gradually the workers began to realize that it was impossible to achieve any lasting advances as long as their actions were limited to economic demands, even if they did thereby extract isolated concessions from Parliament like the 1833 Factory Act. So the struggle for the democratic franchise once again became the focal point. Most of the leaders of the London Working Men's Association who drew up the programme for the next period in the history of the English working-class movement, the six demands of the People's Charter in 1838, were from the earlier period, like William Lovett, James Watson, and Henry Hetherington. Their goal was the secret ballot for all men, equal parliamentary constituencies, payment for MPs, and annual parliaments – in other words, the complete transformation of England into a democracy. Alongside them was the London Democratic Association which counted among its members

Bronterre O'Brien, the English translator of Buonarroti's *History of Babeuf's Conspiracy for Equality*, which brought the aroma of the French Revolution and the tradition of continental conspiracy into the English working-class movement. A Birmingham petition drawn up, like the Charter, by skilled workers called for essentially the same aims. The trade crisis and mass unemployment from 1839 to 1843 sent the call for the Charter echoing throughout the country.

The Chartist leaders, however, never really succeeded in uniting after the rejection of the Charter by the Commons. United action was hindered by disagreement between two opposing groups in the leadership – the Moral Force Party which favoured long-term agitation and collaboration with bourgeois liberals, and the Physical Force Party which maintained that the decisive weapon was the mass strike, though the mass strikes of 1842 were totally unplanned and took both by surprise. Nevertheless, despite internal disagreements, the 1842 Petition which collected the amazing total of over three million signatures demonstrated the strength of the movement and eventually forced Parliament to make social concessions and to pass the 1842 Mining Act.

The Repeal of the Corn Laws in 1846 was first and foremost a victory of the industrial bourgeoisie over the landowners, but it had roots also in the upper class's fear of Chartism. The Ten Hour Bill had been the economic aim of trade unions and Chartists for years, and the 1847 law limiting the working day to ten hours was the result of the last wave of mass Chartism. After the failure of the great mass demonstrations in April 1848 and the defeat of the continental Revolutions in the same year, Chartism receded. In the first volume of *Capital*, Marx accurately characterized the adoption of the legal working day under the 1847 law as 'the result of a long and more or less hidden civil war between the capitalist and the working classes', in which 'the English factory workers championed the cause of the modern working class as a whole'. For Marx the law marked the first great victory for the political economy of the workers over that of the bourgeoisie. 'The workers,' he said, 'had forced through a law which prevented them from signing themselves and their families into death and slavery.'

These two advances – the Mining Act of 1842 and the Ten Hour

Bill of 1847 – won by the English working-class movement between the two Revolutions of 1830 and 1848 in France, set an example to the continental proletariat. Despite the limited character of the legislation, the English workers had proved, first, that the proletariat could compel the capitalist state to intervene in the workings of the economy, second, that direct struggle led by the unions could bring about concessions in wages policy and lead to the raising of the standard of living and cultural level of the working class, thus counteracting the drift – inevitable without class struggle – to mass immiseration.

Chartism's decline, which accompanied the defeat of the 1848 Revolutions in Europe, could not detract from this positive development. Awareness of the importance of the need for international solidarity between revolutionary democrats and workers had been a determining factor in the later stages of Chartism. Under their secretary, George Julian Harney, the Fraternal Democrats remained in touch not only with émigré revolutionaries in England, but also with revolutionary circles abroad. After the election of the first Chartist member of parliament in June 1847, the Chartists prepared for an international congress which was to have been held in Brussels in October 1848 but which was cancelled because of the Revolution. When their third mass petition was rejected by Parliament in July 1848 (at a time when, on the continent, not only the working class but all democrats had been crushed), the movement began to go into sharp decline. Subsequently the English workers had to survive for a considerable period without their own independent political organizations.

The continental Revolutions of 1848 followed the economic crisis of 1847. After the brief prelude of the Swiss civil war in November 1847, the history of the working-class movement took a new turn with the January 1848 national uprisings in Italy, and culminated in the downfall of the bourgeois monarchy in France on 24 February 1848. In the previous Revolution of 1830, workers and petty bourgeoisie had fought for three days continuously shoulder to shoulder in the Paris streets only to see the bankers and oligarchs, and their king Louis Philippe, usurp their victory. The French working class had not then had sufficient political consciousness to make an independent programme and action possible. Its first big strikes, of the Lyons silk weavers in 1831 and 1834, had been easily crushed. Secret revolutionary organizations like the Carbonari and others modelled on them had been active among students and sometimes workers – especially the craftsmen's apprentices – even before the 1830 Revolution. But only during the bourgeois monarchy that followed did they begin consciously, as Louis Blanc wrote in *The History of Ten Years*, to set the interests of the people against those of the bourgeoisie. The Society of the Friends of the People, Blanqui's Society of Families, and the Society of the Seasons all sprang up in quick succession with a common aim: the armed conquest of political power by a highly disciplined group of conspirators to free the workers from wage slavery. A revolutionary dictatorship established by the victorious conspirators would ensure a democratic education of the people and prepare them for life in a communist society. The proletariat played an increasingly active role in these societies, and internationalism united them with German émigré revolutionaries and apprentices. In 1834 the Germans themselves followed the example of the French and formed the Society of the Despised and the League of the Just.

France's increasing industrialization after 1830, protected by the bourgeois monarchy's tariff policies, sharply accentuated the contradictions between finance bourgeoisie, industrial bourgeoisie, and proletariat. Until then France had been a predominantly agrarian country. Institutionalized politics, from which the workers were in any case excluded by the electoral system, were but a token conflict between the ruling finance aristocracy and the official opposition made up of the industrial and intellectual bourgeoisie. The peasants, proud of their property which they owed to the Revolution, were by far the most numerous class in the country. As for the workers, the majority were still employed in small businesses and lacked the militancy of those in big industry. So it was not surprising that the French workers modelled their behaviour and methods of struggle on Babeuf's Conspiracy, relying entirely on a successful *coup* and the building of a revolutionary democratic dictatorship. Their revolutionary vitality was reflected in their constant preparations for a putsch, culminating in the attempted uprising of 12 May 1839, and it reappeared later in the militancy of the Paris proletariat during the February Revolution in 1848 and later still in the Commune of 1871. Auguste Blanqui, the workers' outstanding leader who died in 1881 after a total of thirty-six years behind bars, commanded an extraordinary authority and his funeral became one of the biggest mass demonstrations of French workers ever seen: two hundred thousand people followed his coffin to the grave. The German League of the Just was among those involved in the catastrophic attempted *coup d'état* in 1839. A number of its most active members, Karl Schapper, Heinrich Bauer, and Joseph Moll, fled to England and in 1840 founded the Workers' Educational Society. This soon included democrats and proletarian émigrés from other nations and, as the Communist Workers' Educational Society, was of great significance in the development of the international working-class movement. It remained in existence until 1917.

Other influences besides this conspiratorial communist movement affected the French working class and sought to uphold the independent activity and class struggle of the proletariat. Without understanding them it is impossible to comprehend the role of the workers in the first phase of the Second Republic; for the social changes of the period of growing capitalist industrialism had produced many theoreticians opposed to the dominant characteristics of the liberal economy. Reacting against the large-scale enterprises of industrial capitalism, Charles Fourier set his hopes on a federation of small, quasi-autonomous co-operatives (*phalanstères*), which bore little relevance to an independent working-class movement and its struggles. More realistic was the system expounded by Count Henri de Saint-Simon who fully appreciated the inevitability of big industrial complexes, and who stood for the joint planning of society by industrialists and workers against the non-producers whom he considered parasites. The influence of both Fourier and Saint-Simon was preserved by their followers and had its effect on sections of the working class and finally on Louis Blanc whose call for *le droit du travail* (the right to work) and *l'organization du travail* (the organization of work) were the chief slogans of the first great independent appearance of the Paris workers, between February and June 1848. Pierre-Joseph Proudhon's theories on credit and on mutualism, on the other hand, only influenced the French working class after the turning point of June 1848.

The workers who – as they first thought – were victorious in February 1848, having forced through the inclusion of the socialist Blanc and the worker Albert in the government, and the creation of the Luxembourg Commission, had already either been hit by, or threatened with, unemployment as a result of the economic crisis of 1847. Hence they considered the most urgent problem to be the state guarantee of the right to work. But this had to be implemented in such a way as to make impossible both a repetition of similar economic disasters and the recent total subordination of economic life to the industrialists. Louis Blanc's *ateliers sociaux* (National Workshops), which anticipated Ferdinand Lassalle's state-aided productive cooperatives, appeared to answer this need.

The National Workshops aimed at the gradual elimination of the capitalist economic and social order by means of a credit system operated by a publicly-owned national bank, to be introduced with the harmonious agreement of all classes. Blanc, in fact, hoped to build a true democracy without class struggle but by a peaceful compromise between the petty-bourgeois democrats and the capitalists represented in the provincial government. However, this hope proved to be unjustified, and Blanqui – its critic – to be more than a mere troublemaker embittered by years of imprisonment. For it was through their own harsh experiences after the February Revolution that the workers eventually learnt that he had understood their real interests more clearly than they had themselves.

The National Workshops of 1848 were only an emergency measure. They offered employment only to those not called up for the Guarde Civile. After the elections to the Constituent Assembly, the disillusioned workers tried to save their revolution by the demonstration of 15 May, and to force Parliament and the government to support the Polish Revolution. But nothing could have been further from the intentions of the petty-bourgeois democrats and bourgeois republicans than the united struggle of European democracy against Russia and Prussia. The 15 May demonstration ended in the utopian attempt to conquer power and resulted in the arrest of the old conspiratorial groups. The decree of 21 June 1848 excluding unmarried workers from the National Workshops provoked a further spontaneous uprising of the Paris workers. The five-day battle which followed decided the outcome not only of the French, but also of the European, Revolution. The liberal bourgeoisie throughout the continent surrendered to feudal reaction and cheered on the massacres of more than three thousand imprisoned workers by General Cavaignac. Karl Marx described this first uprising of the French working-class movement in *Class Struggles in France*, published in 1850. Two years later, in *The Eighteenth Brumaire of Louis Bonaparte*, he analysed the consequences of its defeat – the renunciation of political power by the apparently victorious liberal bourgeoisie in favour of the pocket Napoleon and his 'December clique'.

These two analyses of the situation in France were the work of a young intellectual in the process of creating a new method of studying the philosophy, history and economics of contemporary Europe. At the same time they reflected the initial experiences of the German working-class movement which, because of the industrial backwardness of the states of the German Union, could only develop by joining the working-class movements of England and France. The contradictory conjuncture of the economic and social backwardness of Germany and the social and intellectual development of its more advanced European neighbours turned out to be highly significant for the revolution of working-class ideology. It was a conjuncture parallel to the one which had already led to the dominance of the French Enlightenment over English philosophy and, a few decades later, would lead to the dominance of German classical literature and idealist philosophy over French intellectual life. It was this unevenness of development that produced the necessary conditions for the intellectual flowering of the European bourgeoisie. In the same way, it was the insignificance of the German working-class movement in the first half of the nineteenth century which enabled Karl Marx and Friedrich Engels to become, on the eve of the revolutionary uprisings of 1848, the theoreticians of the consciousness and ideology of the *whole* European working class, and to formulate its aim – the supranational classless society.

After the Hambach Festival, the German epilogue to the 1830 Revolution in France and the social unrest in England, many democratic intellectuals had to emigrate from Germany. Among these were the Göttingen professors, Theodor Schuster and Jakob Venedey. They began to work in Paris with journeymen from Germany and to organize themselves along the lines of the French revolutionary democratic secret societies. In 1836 their League of Outlaws became the League of the Just. After the defeat of the *coup* organized by the Society of the Seasons in May 1839, some of the Germans had to move to London. There they began, in 1840, initially as a legal forum of discussion, the German Workers' Educational Society which later became the Communist Workers' Educational Society. Wilhelm Weitling, a journeyman tailor, had written two books for the Society, *Mankind as it now is and as it should be* (1838) and *Guarantees of Harmony and Liberty* (1842). In them the utopian vision of a communist society was united with a plan for an educative revolutionary dictatorship. The London Workers' Educational Society offered a chance to combine French revolutionary political conspiracy with the openly fought class struggles of the English. Engels was in touch with it in November 1843 and Marx visited it in 1845 while passing through London. After he emigrated to Brussels from Paris in 1847 a German Workers' Society sprang up there as well. The socialist émigrés in both Brussels and London replaced the romantic socialism typified by Weitling with a socialism of a new and more concrete character. The League of the Just had realized the significance of Engels's *Conditions of the Working Class in England* as an analysis of the workers' situation, and had recognized how important both Marx's lectures on *Wage Labour and Capital* and his polemic against Proudhon's *Philosophy of Poverty* were in the development of a proper economic theory of society and its extension beyond pure schematism. As a result, at the Society's Congress in London in the summer of 1847, it changed from being a putschist secret society and became a propaganda organization, adopting the name 'The Communist League'. The Second Congress at the end of 1847 took the next step of inviting Marx to draw up the League's programme, a first draft of which had already been provided by Engels.

The Communist Manifesto appeared in February 1848, just before revolution broke out in France. At that time it only had a small circulation and had no effect on the course of events. However, within a few decades it had become the programme of the working-class movement throughout the world. It outlines the theory of historical materialism with penetrating lucidity and gives a precise summary of the evolution of industrial capitalism, in the course of which, Marx explained, it was the duty of the workers in their respective national states to accelerate the course of revolution towards the building of a classless society. The *Manifesto* closes with the slogan which appears again and again in the programmes of the European working-class movement from 1848: 'Working Men of all Countries! Unite.' As Harold Laski wrote in the foreword to the *Manifesto*'s centenary edition:

Few documents in the history of mankind have stood up so remarkably to the test of verification by the future as the *Communist Manfesto*. A century after its publication no one has been able seriously to controvert any of its major positions.

The Communist Manifesto had appeared on the eve of the revolution which it had foreseen and for which it sought to offer guidelines for the workers. That revolution was defeated. The class struggle in France drove the bourgeoisie throughout Europe to abandon its own aims and seek refuge in the arms of reaction. In Germany, members of the Communist League – Wilhelm Wolf in Breslau, Karl Marx as editor of the *Neue Rheinische Zeitung* in Cologne, and Friedrich Engels during the Baden Uprising – fought alongside extreme bourgeois radicals. Only Stefan Born's Workers' Brotherhood in Berlin gave a foretaste of independent political action by the workers; but it had no impact on the character of the movement as a whole and was unable to influence its outcome. However, the revolutionary militancy of the circle surrounding the *Neue Rheinische Zeitung* and their superiority in matters of strategy had such a strong influence on some of the young intellectuals, like Wilhelm Liebknecht and Ferdinand Lassalle, that they preserved the ideas of the Communist League – even if in somewhat watered down form – for the movement's next phase.

The defeat of the Revolution meant that the League's most important members were again forced into exile. The 1850 boom destroyed all hopes of a new revolution and broke first the unity, then the actual existence of the League. Willich and Schapper returned to the ideas of its more conspiratorial days, but the majority of its central committee in London joined Marx and Engels in outright rejection of such illusions. Prussian police persecution put an end to the League's organizational continuity with the Cologne Communist trial in 1852. On 13 July 1854, Bismarck's Prussian delegate proposed a successful motion in the German Parliament banning all workers' associations. Thus ended the first phase of the history of the German working-class movement. The best contemporary account and analysis of the course of revolution in Germany in 1848–9 was Friedrich Engels's *Revolution and Counter-Revolution in Germany*.

The modern working-class movement had its origins in England. Parallel tendencies had soon shown themselves in France and Germany, culminating in the revolutionary wave that swept over Europe as a result of the economic crisis of 1847. Only slowly and through many contradictions was the working-class movement able to develop an independence of thought and action based on the effort to carry bourgeois-democrat thought to its logical conclusion, to apply it to economic problems, and to overcome the harsh deterioration in living conditions which was the consequence of the early industrial epoch and its ensuing crises. Such political action was almost always undertaken by a small section of the workers either in co-operatives or in trade unions, led generally by intellectuals. These two organizations alone succeeded in developing a lasting independent class consciousness in opposition to the ruling ideology, and those active in them came mainly from the ranks of the skilled workers who had better opportunities to continue their education because of their higher earnings. Those workers who suffered increasing immiseration, on the other hand, were for the moment only able to demonstrate their militancy and vitality at times of crisis. At such nodal points of social history they showed themselves capable of unique spontaneous actions, like the machine-breaking of the eighteenth century and earlier, or in July 1830 in Paris, though then they functioned as the auxiliaries of the bourgeoisie. All this changed when independent, if small, organizations began to form with coherent political and social beliefs, capable of exercising a constant influence over the masses.

The defeats of the independent revolutionary actions of the working class in England and France, and of the revolutionary uprisings led mainly by bourgeois democrats in 1848 in industrially backward Germany, were sealed by the June Days in Paris. The prosperity of 1850 once again stabilized the prevailing distribution of power throughout Europe. At the same time, the consciousness of international solidarity remained awake in what survived of the European working-class movement. It held fast to the belief that pre-revolutionary Europe could not be re-established unchanged and that, under new conditions, a new era in working-class history would begin. The aim of a social democracy – the material improvement of the workers' standard of living by struggle against the capitalists, and the overthrow of class privilege in a classless society – had become the common property of the whole working class. International cooperation was its obvious corollary. This spirit survived when European bourgeois democrats were abandoning their own class solidarity in favour of identification with the existing state. The internationalism of the workers was thus paralleled by growing bourgeois nationalism as inter-state rivalry increased. Thus, the first period in the history of the European working class laid the basis of the development which would follow the new wave of industrialization heralded by the prosperity of 1850.

2

The First International

The period of prosperity which ended the initial advance of the European working-class movement in 1849–50 strengthened the industrial development of England and boosted the spread of the new mode of production in France and Germany. As long as the economic boom lasted, the continental bourgeoisie was prepared to put up with the political *status quo* after the defeat of the 1848 Revolution, even though it was itself more or less totally excluded from a share in political power. The army, bureaucracy, and police of Napoleon III ruled France, and the states of the German Confederation were each under the control of a different collection of princes, feudal aristocrats, and bureaucrats. The working class was no longer capable of independent action; after the Revolution its leaders had either been executed, imprisoned, or exiled. Only in England were the trade unions able to preserve a modicum of organizational continuity.

The 1850 boom continued to thrust industry ever deeper into Europe. From 1850 to 1880 steam-generated horse-power in England increased from 1·3 million per annum to 7·6 million, in France from barely ·4 million to 1·3 million, in the German Confederation (afterwards the German Reich) from ·26 million to over 5·1 million, and in the Austrian Empire from ·1 to 1·6 million. Coal production in England went up in the same period from 49 to 147 million tons per annum, in France from ·8 to 3·8 million tons, and in Germany from 1·3 to 12 million tons. Consumer and manufacturing industries showed similar tendencies. The railways were opening up Europe.

The lull in social and political activity in the mid nineteenth century was deceptive. As long as there was uninterrupted economic prosperity, the post-revolutionary order concealed its class contradictions. However, as soon as economic recession set in and prompted the liberal bourgeoisie to begin interfering in the state's internal and foreign policies, the working class also began to play a bigger role. The leading German democrats who had emigrated to Switzerland and England were divided, mainly because each one thought that he represented the course of history in his own individual actions. Such rivalries and differences among the Germans, which destroyed the Communist League, characterized relations between continental political émigrés in those days just as they did relations between Russian revolutionaries later – before 1905 and 1917 – and between political refugees from Italy in the 1920s and Germany in the 1930s. The majority emigrated to North America and were lost to the European working-class movement. In the apparently hopeless situation, only very few had, like Marx and Engels, the ability to turn to research in order to establish a theory for the movement.

In the period of prosperity after 1850, the material conditions of substantial sectors of the industrial workers had improved, although their relative share of total industrial production remained the same. The first curbs on the possibilities of limitless exploitation in the era of primitive capital accumulation were not introduced with the voluntary agreement of the employers but under pressure from the workers. The English Factory Acts of 1833, which initially applied only to the textile industry, established a fixed working day – twelve hours for those between the ages of thirteen and eighteen, eight for children from nine to thirteen, and the abolition of work for children under nine. The employers did their best to evade this law and succeeded in persuading the Commons to reduce the minimum age for child labour to eight years and in making the generally established twelve-hour day for factory work the norm for children as well. However, new advances by the Chartists culminated in the adoption of the Factory Act of 8 June 1847 which cut working hours for women and children first to eleven, then – from 1 May 1848 – to ten hours. The industrialists hit back immediately. But in 1850 the ten-hour day was established for all, though it was at first only legally enforced in the textile industry. Forty years before, when Robert Owen had called for the ten-hour day, the ruling class, on the basis of established economic doctrine, had pronounced it an atheistic violation of the 'Christian' concept of the virtue of work, and had branded it a utopian absurdity. Now it was the law of the land. It was the example of this struggle in England which helped the French workers establish the official twelve-hour day in France – the most important outcome of the February Revolution in 1848.

In periods of industrial prosperity, these first social advances enabled the skilled workers to extract some benefits from the rivalry between employers for the purchase of their labour-power. It is notable that in periods of economic boom, if labour-power is scarce, not even the institutionalized terror of a Third Reich can hold wages down completely, and the Bonapartist regime in France was far from resorting to such methods, however much it suppressed democracy and any signs of political ambition among the workers. Its tactic was to grant certain social concessions to the working class – industrial arbitration, subsidized welfare organizations, and non-political con-sumer cooperatives – in order to reconcile the workers to the system and thus prevent the re-emergence of class consciousness.

When the next crisis occurred, the working class in France and Germany was no longer the small minority it had been before 1848, and some sections of it were materially and culturally somewhat better off. The French and German governments were forced to reduce child labour and to grant workers at least a minimal educa-tion, essential if they were to operate the complicated new machinery. Thus, any new economic crisis was bound to see the appearance of a working-class movement politically and socially stronger than before.

The crisis came in 1857. After the Crimean War and the wars in Italy, both the nationally oppressed Poles and Italians went into action again, reviving democratic sentiments of solidarity towards them elsewhere. The American Civil War provoked Radicals in the English Parliament, and especially English workers, to come out in sympathy with the North and prevent England entering the war as an ally of the South. English workers had won a great victory even earlier. Thanks to the solidarity of the unions throughout the country in forming a strike fund, the London Building Workers' strike of 1859, to which the employers had reacted with lockouts and the suspension of the right to combine on their premises, ended after nine months in the forcing through of a law guaranteeing the right to combine. Such demonstrations of solidarity had led to local alliances among the specialized unions, and meant that the English working-class movement was once again a cohesive force. The struggle for equal voting rights was rejoined, supported by some bourgeois radical members of Parliament. The result was Disraeli's Reform Bill of 1867 and Gladstone's Third Reform Act in 1884 which together enfranchised the majority of both the urban and rural workers.

The 1857–8 crisis also reawoke the French working class. Despite anti-combination laws, a wave of strikes broke out against wage cuts. Then, to prove their goodwill towards the workers, the French government sent a delegation of five hundred and fifty workers to the World Exhibition in London in 1862. Among the delegation, elected by the workers, were a number of Proudhonists, led by Henry-Louis Tolain. In London, they met the London Trades Council and agreed on a joint demonstration, to be held in London on 22 July 1863, in support of the Polish Revolution. The day after, discussions were opened on the possibility of forming a permanent international working men's alliance. The English formed a committee, led by George Odger, which drew up an appeal to the French workers calling for united action by workers in all economically advanced countries, support for the Polish Uprising, and action against English employers who forced down wages by using cheaper continental labour.

The first meeting took place on 28 September 1864 in St Martin's Hall, London. Besides the English and the French, many émigré groups were represented, the Italians by one of Garibaldi's aides, the Germans by members of the Communist Workers' Educational Society. Karl Marx was elected as one of the German members on the Central Committee which initially consisted of thirty-two members. Despite his considerable doubts about the movement's intellectual maturity, Marx considered the Association of the utmost importance. On 29 November 1864 he wrote to his friend Ludwig Kugelmann:

> The Association is important because it includes the leaders of the London trade unions which gave Garibaldi such a momentous reception here and which

defeated Palmerston's plan for a war against America with a giant rally in St James's Hall. The leaders of the Paris workers are also connected with the Association.

In drafting the statutes and the preamble formulating the general principles of the new organization, Marx was able to establish his views over those of the Owenites and the followers of Mazzini. His 'Address to the Working Class', the inaugural address of the International, contained only those ideas to which the trade unions, but also the Proudhonists and Mazzinians, could agree. Taking the ideas of the workers' leaders from each country as his starting point, and stressing what they had in common, Marx aimed to steer a course which would enable them to obtain broader theoretical insight and clarity while fighting their own particular struggles. The whole movement's point of departure, the necessity for united working-class struggle, came clearly and fully to the fore. It was only possible for Marx to incorporate the political and social theories of *The Communist Manifesto* of 1848 in the programme in a limited form, although he did succeed in preventing the mutualist ideas of the French Proudhonists, or the illusions of Mazzini, from setting its tone. Marx's draft for the statutes and Address of the International was accepted unanimously with only minor amendments. The preamble itself is one of the historic documents of the European working-class movement. It runs:

Considering,

That the emancipation of the working classes must be conquered by the working classes themselves; that the struggle for the emancipation of the working classes means not a struggle for class privileges and monopolies, but for equal rights and duties, and the abolition of all class rule;

That the economic subjection of the man of labour to the monopoliser of the means of labour, that is the sources of life, lies at the bottom of servitude in all its forms, of all social misery, mental degradation and political dependence;

That the economic emancipation of the working classes is therefore the great end to which every political movement ought to be subordinate as a means;

That all efforts aiming at that great end have hitherto failed from the want of solidarity between the manifold divisions of labour in each country, and from the absence of a fraternal bond of union between the working classes of different countries;

That the emancipation of labour is neither a local nor a national, but a social problem, embracing all countries in which modern society exists, and depending for its solution on the concurrence, practical and theoretical, of the most advanced countries;

That the present revival of the working classes in the most industrious countries of Europe, while it raises a new hope, gives solemn warning against a relapse into old errors and calls for the immediate combination of the still disconnected movements;

For these reasons:

The undersigned members of the committee, holding its powers by resolution of the public meeting held on 28 September 1864, at St Martin's Hall, London, have taken the steps necessary for founding the Working Men's International Association;

They declare that this International Association and all societies and individuals adhering to it will acknowledge truth, justice and morality, as the bases of their conduct towards each other, and towards all men, without regard to colour, creed or nationality;

They hold it the duty of a man to claim the rights of a man and a citizen, not only for himself, but for every man who does his duty. No rights without duties, no duties without rights.

The International could rely for the most part on the English trade unions, which took out collective membership, on donations of various amounts given by individual members, and occasionally on particular unions in other European countries. Despite the enormous influence attributed to it by the bourgeois press and government spies who, ever since the Prussian spy Schieber and the Cologne Communist trial in 1852, seem to have had a consistently distorted concept of truth, the International's General Council never had a strong organization or substantial funds. However, its authority and reputation with the European workers grew steadily until the defeat of the Paris Commune. Its appeals for solidarity succoured many an important working-class struggle, and it helped to clarify and develop the political and social consciousnesses of the workers it represented.

English members of the International belonged to the Reform League which, since February 1865, united bourgeois radicals and trade unionists in the struggle for the democratization of the franchise, and brought about the electoral reform of 1867. In France most members of the International were largely under the influence of Proudhon. But its support and particularly that of the English unions during the lockout of the Paris bronze workers in 1867, and later during the textile workers' strikes in Rouen and Lyons, and the miners' strike in St Etienne, led to a group of French workers, among them Eugène Varlin, accepting the necessity of strikes, social and political action, and the nationalizing of the monopoly-owned means of production. At first the Blanquists stayed away from the International, though Blanqui himself had attended its Brussels Congress in 1868 as an observer. Belgian, Swiss, Dutch, Italian, and Spanish workers joined, as did the leaders of the first Austrian working-class organization. Besides a few individual members in Germany and the émigrés of the London Workers' Educational Society, the International won the moral support of Lassalle's General German Workers' Union, and in due course of the German Social Democratic Workers' Party, founded by Wilhelm Liebknecht and August Bebel in 1869. Thus it succeeded in representing almost all the independent working-class organizations in Europe, and in initiating both their cooperation over a broad field and the mutual discussion of their aims and strategy. In this way it gave the workers of countries which in 1864 had not possessed even the beginnings of independent working-class organizations, the chance to break away from bourgeois liberalism.

The differences between Marx and the Proudhonist French delegates had been clear at the closed London Conference in 1865. At the International's first public Congress in Geneva they became acute. Henceforth it was a characteristic of all the International's congresses that, in the delegations of those countries which were highly developed industrially, Marx's viewpoint – to which a majority of the General Council subscribed and which was supported above all by the English unions – held sway; whereas in the delegations from essentially agrarian countries (Italy, Spain, and initially France), or from areas with small-scale industry (French Switzerland), Proudhonism was dominant, succeeded by the ideas of Bakunin after the Commune in 1871. In so far as its social basis still existed, this difference could still be seen in modern times in the strength of the Iberian Anarchist Federation (FAI) and the anarcho-syndicalist union (the CNT) in the Spanish resistance to France.

Against opposition from the Proudhonists, the trade union movement and its most important weapon – the strike – were recognized at the Geneva Congress in 1899. The Proudhonist proposal – that only manual workers be granted membership of the International – was rejected; its acceptance would have meant the resignation of Marx.

Eventually the Congress voted unanimously for Marx's proposal to raise demands for social and political changes to the *status quo*, to improve the condition of women and children, and to limit the working day to eight hours. The Proudhonists rejected all state interventions in the drawing up of labour contracts. They held that such policies would stabilize the state and imperil social liberty. Opposing him, Marx pointed out that measures to protect the workers could only be implemented 'by transforming social reason into political force':

In the present circumstances, our only way lies in general laws decreed by state power. . . . In putting through such laws the working class does not strengthen the ruling forces. On the contrary, it transforms them from operating against the workers into becoming their agents. It obtains by general acts what it would be pointless to try and achieve by any amount of individual effort.

For Marx the goal of abolishing the capitalist enterprise did not imply that trade unions should not negotiate with employers so long as they existed, nor did the goal of abolishing the bourgeois state imply that workers' parties should not seek to exact concessions from that state so long as they were not in a position to destroy it. Although the French found support for some of their reservations, they had no effect on the principles adopted at Geneva. Henceforth, the trade unions and the non state-aided productive cooperatives were considered 'the levers by which the tyranny of wage labour and capital could be lifted'.

The arguments between the majority of the General Council, influenced by Marx, and the French Proudhonists were repeated at the Lausanne Congress in 1867. The issue at stake was working-class political struggle. The Proudhonists rejected it because they sought to ignore the question of state power and to exclude it from social development. However much they agreed with the majority over the necessity to nationalize the monopolistic branches of industry, in the first place the railways, there was no agreement over the form nationalization should take. How was it possible other than by using state power? Could big units really function if they were owned by small, decentralized cooperatives, as Proudhon implied? Was the system of small peasant-holdings to be retained for ever, despite the development of modern technology? Or was the conversion of land into public ownership, as the Belgian César de Paepe demanded, inevitable? What should the International's attitude be to the European League for Freedom and Peace launched by the bourgeois radicals? Should the working-class campaign for a compulsory national education system and, where one existed, for its democratization? All these questions were either settled by compromise or postponed. Even if the French did draw nearer the ideas of the majority on the General Council, hidden differences remained on many issues. Only at the Brussels Congress in 1868 was a clear commitment made, opposed by the French, to the socialization of the means of production by public coercion. The Congress also hoped to prevent the sharpening of Franco-German differences into war by a 'popular strike' against governments – a policy which was only too quickly to prove over-ambitious.

With the Basle Congress in 1869 the debate on Proudhonism was concluded. A resolution in favour of the public ownership of all land was accepted by 54 votes against only 4. But there were already signs of the differences which were eventually to lead to the dissolution of the First International. The Russian revolutionary, Mikhail Bakunin, had come to Basle as a delegate from Lyons. He had little time either for the stubborn and systematic daily struggle waged by the trade unions for higher pay and shorter working hours to keep up with the changing conditions, or for the political struggle waged by the workers in industrially developed countries for the extension of democratic rights and for social reform. His ideas corresponded to the situation of the workers in countries with little industrial development. This new conflict was first expressed in an argument over the question of the right of inheritance. No less important was to be the appearance in Basle of the German Social Democratic Workers' Party – the first ever national working-class party. It marked a new phase in the history of the European working-class movement which was now characterized by the rapid rise of such parties elsewhere.

The outbreak of war between France and Germany a year after showed that the Brussels' talk of a 'popular strike' did not reflect the real situation. The governments of both countries had no difficulty in convincing their people that they were fighting a defensive war. The International stood alone. The General Council in London provided a revolutionary democratic analysis of the situation, though not a pacifist one. In its address to the workers of the different countries, it upheld the view that the first duty of the French workers was to bring down Napoleon III, and that at the same time the German workers must stop the war, now no longer being fought for the defence of Germany but for the aggrandizement of Prussia. 'If the German working class allows the present war to become more than strictly defensive, victory and defeat will be equally catastrophic.' The Social Democratic Workers' Party deputies in the parliament of the North German Confederation, Wilhelm Liebknecht and August Bebel, reacted by abstaining in the voting on the war credits. The followers of Lassalle voted in favour of them.

Following the capitulation of the French at Sedan, leading to the proclamation of the Third Republic, the Brunswick central committee of the German Social Democratic Workers' Party called for demonstrations to demand an honourable peace with the French Republic, declaring:

In the name of the German Social Democratic Workers' Party and in accordance with the feelings of the German workers, we hereby protest against the annexation of Alsace-Lorraine. In the common interests of France and Germany, and of peace, freedom, and western civilization against Cossack barbarism, the German workers will not tolerate this annexation. We shall remain loyal to our working brothers in all countries, in all struggles, and stand side by side with them for our common aims.

The members of the central committee who made this statement were promptly arrested and charged with high treason. The 'nationalist' hysteria of the German bourgeoisie was so powerful that it eventually swept a majority of the German workers along with it. Nevertheless, henceforth both the German workers' parties – Eisenacher and Lassalleaner – in the North German Parliament responded to the Paris Federation of the International and voted together against war credits and for the renunciation of all annexation.

The London General Council's Second Address was aimed at the French workers. They were told that it would be a desperate folly to seek to overthrow the bourgeois reactionary transition government of the new Third Republic when the Prussian army was at the gates of Paris. The first priority must be the organization of the workers under these new circumstances. The French members of the International followed this advice until the bourgeois government capitulated to the Prussian armies.

Under the terms of the armistice, the French government conceded the capitulation and disarmament of Paris, now under the defence of the National Guard, consisting of workers and petty bourgeois, and also agreed that elections to a National Assembly should be held. The peasants and the bourgeois wanted peace at any price. More than the Prussians they feared both the radical democrat petty bourgeoisie of the capital who, true to their Jacobin traditions, wanted to repeat the Revolutionary wars of 1793 to save France, and the French workers – led partly by Blanquists and partly by members of the International who followed their lead. The National Assembly, in which the supporters of the two royal houses overthrown in 1830 and 1848 constituted a majority, and the French government headed by Thiers, met first in Bordeaux, then in Versailles. Their aim now was to disarm the Paris National Guard once and for all. Their first attempt failed. Led by Eugène Varlin, the Paris workers rallied to support the National Guard. The government's administrative machinery and personnel were forced to leave the capital, whereupon the population voted its own local representatives – the Commune.

The Commune united legislative and executive power. Popular representatives could be recalled by popular vote at any time. The standing army was replaced by the people in arms. Bourgeois Jacobins, Blanquists, the few members of the International, Proudhonists, and other socialists all united in the Commune. In *The Civil War in France*, Marx wrote about its tremendous historical significance. The Commune proved, he wrote, that the 'working class cannot simply lay hold of the ready-made state apparatus and use it for its own ends'. The working class had to break up that apparatus and replace it with a form of society in which popular representation was not divorced from the real structures of productive activity:

> The Commune was to be a working, not a parliamentary, body, executive and legislative at the same time. . . . Instead of deciding once every three or six years which member of the ruling class was to represent and repress the people in parliament, universal suffrage was to serve the people constituted in communes, as individual suffrage serves every other employer in the search for workers, foremen and accountants for his business. . . . From the members of the Commune downwards, public service had to be done at *workmen's wages*. The privileges and the representation allowance of the high dignitaries of the state disappeared along with the dignitaries themselves.

Marx declared that the Commune had taught him the future form of the proletarian state, prior to the withering away of the state itself:

> Its true secret was this: it was essentially a *working-class government*, the result of the struggle of the producing against the appropriating class, the political form at last discovered under which the economic emancipation of labour could be accomplished.

However, despite its advanced political form, the Commune put through reforms (a rent ceiling, a ban on night work) which fell short of such a fundamental emancipation. Despite these self-imposed limitations, the bourgeoisie's hatred remained undiminished. Bismarck placed Napoleon III's captured army at the disposal of Thiers and, on 21 May 1871, it began to march on Paris. After bitter resistance by the National Guard and the workers, government troops took the town after a week. The number of dead and deported has never been accurately determined. The victors themselves spoke of 14,000 fallen or executed Communards, 5,000 deported, and a further 5,000 sent to prison by special courts. For the second time in two and a half decades the French working class lost its most active members.

The two German working-class parties had only been able to organize a minority of the German working class. They were too weak to prevent their government from invading Alsace-Lorraine, thus making national differences between the two leading countries of the continent a key issue of European history and forcing bourgeois France to ally with Tsarist Russia. In this way the German ruling classes sacrificed the real interests of the people to pseudo-nationalism and to its own strong material interests.

The European bourgeois press had tried to blacken the name of the International before the Commune. In Austria, leading workers' representatives like Andreas Scheu and Heinrich Oberwinder were imprisoned for high treason merely for showing sympathy for it. After the Paris events in 1871, bourgeois 'public opinion' reacted with particular ferocity. To justify the massacres, a totally blind eye was turned to the historical facts and the Commune was interpreted as a conspiracy hatched by the General Council of the International. The French government passed an emergency law against the International and tried to persuade other countries to extradite or hunt down émigré Communards. The government of the German Reich and the Hapsburgs intended to convene a conference of European states to fight the International. To this the Spanish government gave a lead after Pope Pius IX had reprimanded the Swiss government in the following terms:

You tolerate that sect of the International which seeks to do in Europe what it did in Paris. These gentlemen of the International are to be feared because they are in league with the eternal enemies of God and mankind.

The Encyclical *Quod apostolici muneris* still adhered to this judgement on the International and socialism when it was issued in 1879. However, this attempt to unite Europe in an anti-socialist Inquisition was ultimately frustrated thanks to the British bourgeoisie's commitment to individual liberty.

Meanwhile, the International itself saw the onset of the conflict on which it was eventually to founder, between the former members of Bakunin's International Democratic Alliance, and the General Council still under the leadership of Marx. The outcome of the struggle in Paris made it impossible to hope for a new wave of democratic revolutions in Europe. The resolution at the London conference in 1871, calling for the foundation of legal working-class parties in each European country as the precondition for socialist revolution, was but the result of this new situation. For the followers of Blanqui and Bakunin this was unacceptable. Both still thought in terms of Europe's pre-industrial past. Neither did this new policy correspond to the needs of the English trade unions which, as the 1868 elections had shown, were still too weak to be able to act as an independent political force. They pinned their hopes instead on an alliance with the radical wing of the Liberal Party, so as to be able to use their votes to improve the social conditions of the workers. Marx and the General Council were isolated. This became clear at the Hague Congress of the International in 1872. Although they could together still win a majority, they no longer received the votes of the English. As a result, the General Council was transferred to the United States, and this was followed by the dissolution of the First International – formally announced in 1876.

The 'anti-authoritarian' Bakuninist opposition set itself up in Switzerland immediately after its defeat at the Hague, claiming to be the only legitimate representative of the old International. Because of their loose organization, the Bakuninists were able to win the temporary support of some Belgian groups and of the German Lassalleaner, besides that of Italian and Spanish anarchists. In 1877 the Bakuninists convened the World Socialist Congress in Ghent, attended by working-class parties which developed in Europe in the meantime. This congress saw a definitive break between the Anarchist International which now no longer represented a mass movement outside the Iberian peninsula, and other socialists. Pronouncements of international solidarity apart, a common organization was no longer possible.

The Hague Congress in 1872 marked the end of the first period in the history of the modern European working class. Through the International Working Men's Association – the First International – it had created the conditions for the next period: the building of national working-class parties throughout Europe, their union in the Second International, and the rise of the trade unions. In the Geneva statement on trade unions in 1866, and the London decisions on the task of working-class parties in 1871, the International laid down the immediate future strategy of the European working class.

3

Working-Class Parties and Trade Unions

By the time the International passed the resolution in 1871 recommending the workers in industrially developed countries to form national working-class parties, there already existed two examples of this new instrument of struggle in Germany. Under the new industrial legislation of the North German Union, the most important preconditions for the development of the trade union movement, the right to combine, had been granted in 1869. However, the two German working-class parties – Lassalle's General German Workers' Union and August Bebel and Wilhelm Liebknecht's Social Democratic Workers' Party – together comprised only a minority of the German working class – which was increasing rapidly as a result of intensive industrialization. In the Reichstag elections of 1874, none of the working-class parties received more than three per cent of the votes; only after their unification as the German Social Democratic Party (SPD) in 1875 at Gotha did their influence increase. By the time of the 1877 Reichstag elections, the united party's share of the vote was already nine per cent. The Anti-Socialist Laws in effect during the following years were able to ban, but not to destroy, the party. After a short crisis of adjustment, its influence increased from election to election even during the years of illegality.

Organizationally the party remained intact. The attempts by a few intellectuals to introduce a conciliatory line were blocked, and anarchist tendencies among some members and former Lassalleaner leaders were quickly overcome. The party rallied to a simplified version of Marxism, though Marx and Engels expressed frequent reservations about the leadership's grasp of scientific socialism – above all in Marx's trenchant *Critique of the Gotha Programme.*

Politically the Party was represented by its illegal central committee, the periodical the *Sozialdemokrat*, edited by Eduard Bernstein, and by Karl Kautsky's legal *Neue Zeit*. The fact that it was the only party to champion equal rights for women, including equal voting rights, gave it a good standing among critical minorities of the educated classes. Following the Imperial edict banning the party promulgated in 1881, the Reich government put through various social measures – accident, sickness, and invalid insurance – designed to forestall the growing influence of social democracy, without, however, having the desired effect. Obstructed though the trade unions were by the emergency laws against them, their position after the spontaneous Miners' Strike in 1889 was unassailable. Thus, legislation against the working-class movement in Imperial Germany came to nothing: the Anti-Socialist Laws were not renewed after 1890.

By organizing and training working-class cadres, mostly from the ranks of the skilled workers, and with the cooperation of socialist intellectuals, German socialism showed that it was strong enough to wrest considerable socio-economic concessions from the government. It was thus able to improve the conditions and the living standards of the whole working class in times of economic prosperity, and to give it some stability in times of crisis. Such success was only possible because, in the first place, the party held fast to its aims of achieving political democracy and a socialist economy, entailing the taking of the important means of production into common ownership; and, secondly, because it consistently exploited all legal forms of struggle, eschewing senseless acts of violence, using parliament as a political platform, elections as a measure of influence, and electoral campaigns for propaganda. It thus ensured the legal activity of its trade union organizations which, unlike the Liberal Hirsch-Duncker unions, recognized the right to strike as an instrument of the class struggle. The publication of the party's policy in the Erfurt Programme in 1891 marked the transformation of a once conspiratorial organization into a mass party. Yet the very success of the party in defending the interests of the workers within capitalism increased the danger of the reformism and political weakness already noted by Marx.

At the time of their united campaign against the Hamburg lockout, organized by the employers against both the right to combine and the 1890 May demonstration, the free – i.e. socialist – unions observed the disadvantage of their fragmentation into countless local professional unions. Accordingly, after the Trade Union Congress in Halberstadt in 1892, each profession was centralized in a single union which was in turn incorporated in a central body. The relatively weak localist opposition to this was a trade union counterpart to the opposition of the Social Democratic youth. Together they represented those groups who did not understand, and had not made, the transition from semi-legality under the Anti-Socialist Laws to open and legal struggle alongside the majority of the working class, and they formed the embryo of German anarcho-syndicalism which remained almost totally without influence.

The German trade unions grew quickly. In 1892 they only had 300,000 members; by 1899 they numbered 600,000 (including the weaker Christian unions), and by 1912 two and a half million. The majority of their officials were simultaneously in the Social Democratic Party. Around both organizations were grouped numerous cultural and sporting associations and clubs. It was now possible, at least for unionized workers, to raise the level of wages, except when there was an economic recession. From the end of the nineteenth century, pay agreements between unions and employers were of increasing significance. The rival organization supported by the authorities, the Christian National Trade Union, was only able to form mass organizations in exclusively Catholic areas where religion held sway. To remain in existence they too had to adopt the weapon of the strike, despite their initial resistance to it.

As a result of the success of the German workers' party and of the trade unions connected with it, both were widely regarded as models for the working-class movements of other European countries.

The growth of Austrian social democracy took a similar course to that of Germany, though it was more beset by conflicts and experienced more decisive setbacks. In December 1869 a demonstration in Vienna forced through the right to combine. In 1872 the Austrian Social Democratic Party was formed and spread quickly to the industrial centres of the multi-national state. This multi-national structure of the Austrian state in turn multiplied the problems of social democracy. Moreover, for the German-speaking workers, the Slavs – above all the Czechs and the Slovaks – were still burdened with the counter-revolutionary role they had played in 1848-9. The vague formula of the self-determination of nations adopted by the Austrian party was sufficient to obscure national differences in 1872. The differences, on the other hand, between the moderates under Heinrich Oberwinder and the radicals under Andreas Scheu, between the strategy of conducting a struggle for reforms in alliance with the liberal bourgeoisie against a feudal bureaucratic aristocracy, and conducting an outright, independent class struggle, could not be so obscured. In 1874 the leaders of both factions emigrated. From 1881, under the leadership of Joseph Peukert, the Viennese workers increasingly adopted anarchist methods. This destroyed their unity and obliterated the socialist influence on the Austrian working class, although in the industrial centre of Bohemia and Moravia development was less erratic.

Only at the very end of 1889, at the Hainfeld Party Congress, did Victor Adler succeed in overcoming this fragmentation on the basis of a declaration of Marxist principles acceptable to all. Henceforth, membership of the Austrian Social Democratic Party, and the number of its supporters, increased. In November 1905 it organized the great mass strike for voting rights without which the 1907 electoral reforms would have been impossible. The division of labour between the party, the unions, and the cooperatives, and the structure of the workers' associations in the movement, were based on those of Germany.

In the other half of the Dual Monarchy, Hungary, the beginnings of industrialization were at first restricted to Budapest. For a long time, the small socialist and revolutionary democratic groups there remained isolated and the power of the feudal landlords unbroken. The unions united in 1880 and adopted a socialist programme. Only in 1890 was a socialist party created, based on that of Austria.

It took some time for the French working class to recover from the defeat of the Commune. The economic crisis of 1873-4 which accelerated the rise of German social democracy did not work to the advantage of the organizational beginnings of French socialism. The outstanding working-class leaders had either been killed, imprisoned, or forced into emigration, and the working-class movement was only able to reconstitute itself at the time of the 1879 economic crisis, after the amnesty of the Communards. In the same year, Jules Guesde's Federation of Socialist Workers was formed in Marseille and in 1880 adopted a programme drafted by Guesde and Paul Lafargue and written by Karl Marx. Its content to a great extent anticipated the Austrian Hainfeld and the German Erfurt programmes. But as early as 1882 a split opened in the new French party. The Possibilists under Paul Brousse – from whom within a few years the supporters of Jean Allemane split further – wanted to pursue a systematic policy of electoral alliances with the bourgeois democrats and were in favour of a federal solution for France. In this way they hoped to realize their socialist goals step by step, by evolutionary reformist methods and without conquering state power. Very soon the Blanquists also reorganized themselves as an independent party under the leadership of Éduard Vaillant.

This fragmentation of French socialism was partly the result of the internal political situation in the first phase of the Third Republic, from 1871 to 1879, when the constitution only remained unchanged for so long because the two powerful monarchist groupings could not agree on whether the ruling dynasty should be Bourbon or Orleanist. However, despite its organizational chaos, the influence of the French working-class movement constantly increased. In 1884 the ban on combinations was lifted from the 'Code Civil' and only two years later the National Federation of Trade Unions was formed with the help of Guesde's French Workers' Party. Nevertheless, in France too, sharp differences soon opened up in the trade union movement between a Marxist minority which wanted to follow the Germans in combining parliamentarian and trade union activity, and a syndicalist majority which placed its hope only in direct action – the general strike – as well as an orthodox Proudhonist anti-political minority. Despite the growing gap between the socialist parties and the trade unions, the living standards of the French industrial proletariat improved like the others. However, social legislation proceeded slowly. Comprehensive social insurance for the miners was introduced in 1894, and accident insurance in 1898.

In Italy industrialization had been gradual. The beginnings of the

Italian working-class movement were influenced by the traditions of the national democratic revolution. Conspiracies and putsches were more familiar to it than systematic, legal struggle in the political arena and in the trade unions. In 1872 the Italian section of the International was so strongly under the influence of the Bakuninists that it boycotted the Hague Congress and joined Bakunin's 'anti-authoritarian' International. In the 1873-4 economic crisis it attempted putsches in Bologna and other big towns, but nowhere was it able to win the support of substantial numbers of the proletariat or of the working population. In 1877 an attempted putsch, led by Cafiero and Malatesta, was repeated in the southern village of Letino, providing the government with a welcome opportunity to attack not only the anarchists but their legal socialist rivals. It was to be many years, after the increased industrialization of the North, the attempt to form a small social reformist party, and the founding of the Italian socialist periodical *La Critica Sociale* in 1892, before the Italian Socialist Party was formed. Peasant uprisings and the strike of the sulphur miners in Sicily led, in 1894, to an Italian version – equally unsuccessful – of the German Anti-Socialist Laws. Police violence against a Sicilian miners' strike provoked a mass strike in the North, led by the left of the party and the unions under Arturo Labriola. As a result, the Giolitti government was forced to renounce all use of military force against strikes.

The growth of the Spanish working-class movement was beset by similar problems. The industrialization of Spain was even further behind that of Italy, so the anarchist influence remained stronger. The contrast between, on the one hand, the Iberian Anarchist Federation (FAI) and the anarcho-syndicalist National Workers' Federation (CNT) which were both first and foremost parties of the rural and unskilled workers, and the General Union of Workers (UGT) consisting of Austrian miners and skilled industrial workers, on the other, has remained until the present day in the illegal opposition to the Franco regime. The UGT was supported by the Spanish Socialist Party founded by Pablo Iglesias in 1879. The conflicts which followed the defeats of the bourgeois revolution in 1868 reinforced the aversion felt by large sections of the Spanish working class for all legal and particularly parliamentary forms of struggle. The suppression of Basque and Catalan minorities by the Madrid regime increased the federalist tendencies of working-class organizations, while the almost medieval social role and mentality of the Catholic bishops and monasteries, coupled with the Church's substantial landownership, made intense and sometimes violent anti-clericalism an inevitable ingredient of intellectual freedom. For all these reasons, Spain has remained the only European country in which a substantial anarchist movement has survived into the present day.

In the same period the working-class movement also began to develop in the smaller countries. Industrialization came early to Belgium. At first Bakuninism and Blanquism flourished among the Walloon-speaking workers, whereas in the Flemish-speaking part of the country German social democracy was the model. In 1884 the two united and the economic crisis of the eighties led to the great strike of 1886 which mobilized the Walloon workers in favour of equal voting rights. The strike was smashed by the army, whereupon the Blanquists split off from the party again and tried to repeat it in 1888. In 1889 unity was finally restored between the different political, cooperative and trade union groups, on a federal basis within a single party. The year 1892 saw a further general strike for the franchise. Only a third general strike led to an increase in those entitled to vote, although the upper classes retained their domination over the Senate and had the advantage of a plural vote. At the same time, the strikes of 1886, 1892 and 1893 had had their effect and brought with them the first social and economic advances. From 1894, the Belgian workers' party led by Émile Vandervelde and Edouard Anseele had an important parliamentary faction.

The history of the Netherlands followed the general pattern: a gradual improvement of the workers' economic condition only came through state intervention, prompted by the action of the workers. A strong trade union and political working-class movement acted as a counter to the fluctuations of the general economic situation. The initial advance of the Dutch working class ended with the defeat of the Paris Commune. A fresh start was made with the creation of the Socialist League in 1881 by the Christian Socialist and former priest, Domela Niewenhuis, elected to parliament in 1888 despite the undemocratic franchise. In 1889 parliament at last turned to the problem of state intervention in matters of employment and social insurance, though it eventually ended by postponing its solutions – even then only provisional ones – over a decade. This converted Niewenhuis to direct action and turned him against parliamentarism. A social democratic party was formed in 1894 under the leadership of P. J. Troelstra and H. van Kol. Modelling itself on the German Social Democratic Party, it soon became an important force.

Denmark was the first among the Scandinavian countries to show the beginnings of an independent working-class movement. The Building Workers' Strike in 1871 ended in mass arrests and an emergency law aimed against the International. The political police were able to prevent these beginnings from stirring again by forcing the workers' leaders into exile with heavy fines. Nevertheless, in 1880, the local unions and political workers' associations, which had grown up as a result of increasing industrialization, succeeded in uniting to form a single party which already numbered 20,000 members in 1889.

The ideas of the working-class movement were brought to Sweden and propagated, particularly among the timber workers, by August Palm who had worked as a craftsmen's apprentice in Germany; he was joined by Hjalmar Branting. A Social Democratic party based on the Danish, which also included the trade unions, was formed in 1889. An independent trade union federation was formed considerably later, in 1898.

In Norway the working-class movement had its origins in the democratic traditions of 1848. A trade union federation was formed in 1883, a workers' party in 1887. At that time, Norway and Sweden were united, and the Norwegian working class adopted the Marxism of German social democracy.

In Switzerland the initial Bakuninist influence in the French, Romansh, and Italian-speaking cantons had waned. In the long run Bakuninism proved inappropriate to the political climate of a petty-bourgeois country which had fought to establish a durable democratic constitution. In 1873 the unions united under Hermann Greulich to form the Swiss Workers' Association, and in 1878 the Grütli-Verein, a bourgeois radical organization active since 1838 in patronizing the

welfare of the sick, and workers' education, extended its commitment to making reformist socialist demands. The Workers' Association joined the Swiss Social Democratic Party, founded in 1888, and
together they adopted the Marxism of the social democratic parties
of other European countries, although the fact that Switzerland was
a functioning bourgeois democracy with a strong petty-bourgeoisie
and middle-class peasantry exercised a permanent influence on the
ideology of its working class.

The Polish workers were forced to build up their organizations
under much more difficult conditions. Poland was divided between
Prussia, Russia, and Austria, and whereas the Polish upper class
gave up the idea of national independence after the defeat of the 1863
uprising, the young working-class movement, particularly in Russian
Poland, identified with and continued the revolutionary democratic
tradition. The first attempt, in 1882, to create a centralized secret
organization ended in catastrophe and mass arrests. In 1892 the
Polish Socialist Party was founded in Paris. It was able to hold its
First Congress in Warsaw in 1894. Led by Joseph Pilsudski, it strove
to establish a sovereign and democratic Polish state and claimed to
unite this nationalist aim with working-class interests and the aims of
the international working-class movement. The Yiddish-speaking
workers, on the other hand, united in 1897 in the Bund which regarded itself as a branch of Russia's revolutionary socialist movement
and took part in the founding congress of the Russian Social Democratic Workers' Party in 1898. The Polish Marxist intellectuals and
those workers under their influence dreamed of a social democratic
Russian federal republic in which all people, including the Poles,
would be given national autonomy. They joined forces with the
social democrats of Russian Poland and formed the basis of the
Polish and Lithuanian Social Democratic Party (SKDPiL) founded
in 1900 under the leadership of Leon Jogiches and his pupil Rosa
Luxemburg.

Like the Bund, this party, too, felt itself part of the young
working-class movement of the Tsarist Empire whose industrialism
was just beginning. However, neither Herzen's translation of the
Communist Manifesto, nor Nikolai Davidson's of the first volume of
Capital in 1872, could at first prevent the Narodniks in Russia from

setting their hopes on terrorism and agrarian socialism instead of on the organization of the workers. Only in 1883, as émigrés in Geneva, did Georg Plekhanov, Paul Axelrod, Vera Zasulich, and Leo Deutsch found the Marxist 'Emancipation of Labour' Group, which established the theoretical basis for the formation of social democratic and trade union centres in Russia at a time when the growth of industry was creating a significant working class. As a result, even though many delegates and party workers were arrested after the founding congress of the Russian Social Democratic Workers' Party (RSDP) in 1898 in Minsk, the party could no longer be completely destroyed.

The wave of industrialization which followed the Franco-Prussian war established conditions in most European countries for the growth of independent working-class parties and trade unions. The same supranational social problems led them to political internationalism and the traditions of the International. At the same time, the national tensions in Europe were on the increase. It was this that almost inevitably led to the formation of a new International.

4

The Second International up to the First World War

The new national working-class parties were united in their aim of transforming capitalist society into a classless society and they faced similar problems in their various different countries. All wanted to broaden the base of political power, to improve work conditions and wages, and to insure the workers against sickness, disability, and unemployment. The forms of struggle – union-led strikes and the organization of the workers into trade unions and political parties – followed similar patterns. Everywhere political pressure on the bourgeois was an important means of supplementing the actions of the trade unions in struggling to ensure that the workers' living standard kept pace with technical progress and the resulting steep rise in productivity. Such pressure was also capable of bringing about more tolerable conditions for whose who – either temporarily, through sickness and unemployment, or permanently, through disability and old age – were forced to retire from work. Despite growing political differences between the governments of their countries, the working-class parties pressed for a new international organization, if only because of the need to exchange experiences and coordinate activity at an international level. However, the working-class movement still had unsolved national problems, for instance in Poland and in the Austro-Hungarian Empire. But an identity between national liberation and international solidarity had already characterized the movement from its early days. Although the difficulties in Poland and Czechoslovakia brought tactical problems, the differences were not fundamental and cannot be said to have been an insuperable obstacle to the rebuilding of the unity of the European working class. A much more serious threat to internationalism was posed by the ability of the major capitalist states to attract the support of sections of the working class for their imperialist ambitions. It was particularly difficult to wean away workers from loyalty to their own bourgeois state when that state could offer them reforms and economic concessions.

After the First International, international workers' conferences had been held, in Ghent (1877), in Chur (1881), and in Paris (1883 and 1886) at the invitation of the French Possibilists, and in 1888 in London at the invitation of the British trade unions. However, only some sections of the working-class movement attended these meetings. On the hundredth anniversary of the storming of the Bastille (14 July 1889) two competing conferences were held in Paris. Urged on by the trade unions, the Possibilists had mainly invited union leaders; at the same time, the Guesdists staged a counter congress. No agreement was reached to unite the two. The representatives of the major European working-class parties, as well as delegates from the United States and Argentina, attended the congress organized by the Marxist followers of Guesde, and it was they who initiated the re-establishment of the International. It was decided to hold a demonstration in all countries on 1 May 1890 for the introduction of the eight-hour day, and that this demand should be made not only of the employers but of the bourgeois state itself.

From the time of these congresses the emphasis of the International lay in Europe. Because of America's different class structure and the different problems associated with it, the American delegations did not play a decisive part in any of the International's congresses. The same can be said of the few delegates from working-class organizations in Asia. The Indian delegates represented rather a nation suffering colonial oppression than a workers' movement, and those who represented the semi-legal working-class movement in Japan – a country undergoing intensive industrialization but which was still under feudal militaristic rule – spoke only for a still politically insignificant minority. The International remained oblivious to this discrepancy between its universal claims and its narrowly European base.

The period of the First Congress of the Second International was still characterized by conflict with the anarchist minority who fundamentally rejected the struggle for state-sponsored social legislation and rejected any participation in parliament. The London Congress in 1896 finally put an end to these differences. It was decided in future only to invite representatives of those organizations working to change capitalism into socialism and which recognized the value of legislation and parliamentary activity. All anarchists were therefore excluded, a decision which reflected the general development of national working-class movements. Outside Spain, the anarchists dwindled into small isolated groups; only in the Netherlands, Italy, and in the French unions were they still able to make an impact.

At the Paris Congress in 1900 the Second International formed the administrative apparatus necessary for the international co-ordination of all its members. An International Secretariat, an International Socialist Office, and an Interparliamentary Committee were established. The Secretariat was in Brussels and its first president was Émile Vandervelde. The International Socialist Office consisted of two delegates from each member party.

Nevertheless, despite its organization, the International continued to reflect the development of the different parties belonging to it. It was a vehicle for the debates between the different groups, and it internationalized their internal discussions. Although seldom itself able to influence individual parties, it was able to make an important contribution towards the unification of the socialists in France.

The twenty-five years which preceded the First World War, when the Second International was in its prime, were characterized by renewed industrial prosperity. Production rose in all industrialized countries, and those where industrialization had barely, or had only just, begun were incorporated into the capitalist system. In the German Reich, for instance, the total annual value of industrial production had doubled between the foundation of the Reich in 1871 and 1890, and between then and 1913 it increased again by a hundred per cent. These were the years of new giant industries and of the rise of the electrical and chemical concerns which transformed the means of production throughout Europe and were at the root of uneven industrial development. Whereas the manufacture of the means of production increased tenfold in this period, the increase in production of consumer goods was much slower. Nor was this in

any sense peculiar to the relatively young German industrial capitalism; it was paralleled in the general tendency of European development, resulting in the advent of a new imperialist phase of European
capitalism. In 1890 German exports were still increasing at an annual
rate of 2·3 per cent. On the other hand, the growth rate rose ten per
cent annually up to the outbreak of the war, while imports remained
stable at less than half this amount. In this respect, too, Germany
only offered a particularly clear example of the changes undergone
by advanced European capitalism in these years. The same could be
said for the protectionist policy of supporting heavy industry and
agriculture, introduced in Germany in 1878. The export of capital
to the relatively backward European and non-European countries
and to the colonies under direct European rule constantly increased.
In the previous phase of industrialization this had been predominantly an English and French phenomenon: in 1880 German capital
investments abroad comprised probably only a third and a fifth of the
French and English totals respectively. The new wave of industrialization increased both the unevenness of development and the pace
of expansion. By 1914 German investments abroad were already
half those of the French and a third of the English. The rivalry of the
capitalist classes of the great industrial nations of Europe was bound
to sharpen into political and military conflict between the states
representing them.

As Marx had predicted, the concentration and centralization of
capital proceeded, promoted by the changes in the means of production. In the German Reich, for instance, the electric industry was
dominated by two concerns – AEG (the General Electricity Company)
and Siemens; the chemical industry was similarly controlled by two
groups who were moreover united by countless patent agreements;
and the iron and steel industry was in the hands of a few cartelized
family businesses. Banking was more or less totally under the control of
five giant banks. The liberal competitive capitalism of the pre-1890s
had been forced to give way surprisingly quickly to the modern oligopolistic capitalism and imperialism, in which the free market played
only a secondary role. Joseph Chamberlain's conversion from free
trade to protectionism and colonialism was a striking demonstration
of the structural changes undergone throughout the capitalist world.

Although other European countries did not experience a development as swift as that of Germany, they were moving in the same direction. This produced changes in the political aims of the European big powers. As a result partly of the direct pressure of certain large-scale capitalist interests – particularly heavy industry – and also partly because a capitalist economy which relies on the politically supported export of capital and on the domination of the markets of subject and colonial countries is forced to expand, the rivalry between the big powers for weapons and military equipment became a headlong arms' race.

At the same time, the share of the public sector in the social product grew, and the number of employees among the working population of the industrial countries increased, while the number of independent small businessmen, craftsmen and, to a lesser extent, peasants decreased. Within the ranks of the employees, the numbers not only of white-collar workers but also of technicians rose more quickly than the number of ordinary workers. The extension of state control as a result of social and armaments' programmes increased the number both of civil servants and of those employed by public bodies and in administration.

In this period wage levels rose in relation to the cost of living. This is again best exemplified by Germany. From 1890 to 1900 the cost of living remained essentially stable. With the beginning of the arming of the fleet and the onset of the general arms' race – in other words, with the total commitment by the big powers to imperialism – the cost of living went up and the value of money down.

If one takes 100 as the cost of living index (food, clothes, rent) of a German working-class family of five, this figure underwent marginal alterations up to 1900, reflecting the changes in the economic situation. After the 1901–2 economic crisis, however, it rose to 130 in 1913–14. Between 1890 and 1900, the average wage rose eight to ten per cent, constituting a genuine improvement in the standard of living, only interrupted by the economic crisis of 1891–2. But after 1900 every wage rise meant only the maintenance of this level and marked an actual improvement only if it went beyond merely compensating for the decline in the purchasing power of money. This was precisely what, up to the outbreak of the war, certain groups of workers were unable to achieve; for instance, the relatively highly unionized printers, metal workers, and miners who were among the best paid workers at the turn of the century. The situation was naturally no better for the badly organized workers – those on the land and in the textile industry. However, there were groups who, thanks to thoroughgoing unionization, were able to improve their situation. In Germany this was true first and foremost of the timber workers and the builders, where the concentration of capital had not progressed quite so far as in other industries. In general, however, productivity – and therefore profits – rose faster than wages. Trade union pressure, now making itself felt more and more because of the increasing significance of wage agreements, led to a gradual reduction of the average length of the working day. Nevertheless, the eight-hour day, the aim of the founding congress of the Second International, was achieved nowhere.

This change in the structure of European and world capitalism underlay both the activity of the workers' parties which united in the Second International, and the emergence of the united national trade unions, which since 1901 had formed an International Conference of Trade Unions, and since 1903 an International Secretariat. At the same time, the improvement in the standard of living and the social security of the working class, however small and however far behind the increase in productivity, was not an automatic development but the result of class struggle waged by the socialist parties and trade unions. The working-class organizations had become simultaneously object and subject of social progress, even if rapid growth and success led them all too often to theoretical overestimation of their own role.

The prototype for the parties of the Second International and for the trade unions of the International Trade Unions Organization was the German working-class movement which continued to grow impressively in the period following the foundation of the Second International. In 1912 the free trade unions in Germany numbered 2,553,000 members; on the eve of the First World War, the SPD had over 1,086,000 members, counted 4,250,000 votes (34 per cent of the total), and had 110 parliamentary representatives. No German town was without its social democratic daily paper, its consumer cooperative, its workers' sports club and cultural associations. The great popular orators of the early years of the movement (Wilhelm Liebknecht and Paul Singer) were no longer alive and August Bebel died in 1913. Clara Zetkin was the last surviving representative of a generation which had sat at the feet of Friedrich Engels and been taught not only how to lead a vast organization, but also the fundamentals of the class struggle. Was it then conceivable that the organizational strength of German social democracy was not paralleled by political strength? After all, had not Karl Kautsky, its leading theoretician, developed Engels's inheritance since his death in 1895 as Engels had that of Marx after his death in 1883? Had not the party adopted clear strategic principles in its Erfurt Programme? Had not the rejection of Eduard Bernstein's revisionism at the 1899 and 1903 party conferences proved that the party had avoided the danger of adjusting to Wilhelmine military monarchism? Would the party not heed the argument advanced by Engels who in 1891 pointed out that a capitalist class society might conceivably be overcome by peaceful methods in England, France, and America, but not in the Hohenzollern, Hapsburg, or Romanov empires?

As a result of this record, the authority of the SPD in the Second International remained unchallenged. Even the most consistent revolutionaries, the Bolshevik faction of the RSDP led by Lenin, took – prior to 1914 – the German Party's pseudo-revolutionary politics seriously, and Kautsky's Marxist scholasticism for real Marxism.

Nevertheless, the contradiction in Germany between appearance and reality, between the purely organizational power of both the SPD and the trade unions, and their lack of militancy, had long been evident. Organizationally the party had generated a whole category of parliamentarians, working-class bureaucrats and functionaries in the trade unions, the cooperatives, the party secretariats, the editorial offices of the party press, and as parliamentary delegates. Such people no longer lived *for*, but also *off* the working-class movement. Like all bureaucrats, they were proud of their domains, particularly of every little success they were able to achieve within the conventional and traditional routine. For them, the organization of the movement had changed from being a lever of action to an end in itself. They were unaware that ends and means had changed places in their minds, and were suspicious of any action by the masses which overstepped the 'legal framework' and endangered the movement's legality. Unfortunately the SPD became the model for other European working-class parties in this, as in other respects. Nevertheless in Germany, these bureaucrats were bound to accept and to tolerate the party's continual invocations of capitalism's eventual decline and the working class as its inheritor: such language was important for bringing new sections of the working class into the party and increasing its membership and votes. However, according to the leaders, the party should indeed only be heir to, not the catalyst of, such a decline.

In the trade unions these problems were still more complicated. Every major strike placed the trade union bureaucrats before decisions for which they did not feel adequate. The mass strikes by the German miners in 1889 and 1905 did not originate in the trade unions. In 1905 the unions even tried to force the strikers to withdraw prematurely at a time when the party still supported the strike. And in the same year, Karl Legien – one of the leaders of the German unions – claimed that 'general strikes are general nonsense', just when the miners were forcing concessions from the government by their mass strike, and a general strike in Russia had triggered off the attempted revolution of 1905.

Supported by a majority at the Party Conference, Bebel successfully rejected Bernstein's thesis of the incompatibility of reform and revolution, pointing out their dialectical unity in the daily struggle. Nevertheless, Jean Jaurès was right when he told Bebel at the Amsterdam Congress of the Second International in 1904 that the striking difference between the voting strength and the real power of the SPD was a corollary of the gap between its radical phraseology and its inability to act, which had been evident in its acceptance of the suspension of the general franchise in Saxony.

As long as an outwardly peaceful balance remained between the imperialist great powers, and there were no major social or political conflicts, the SPD and the German unions proved to be powerful organizations, able to win numerous concessions for the workers by their very pressure alone. However, every crisis that arose only revealed the feet of clay on which this colossus really stood.

The 1905 revolution in Russia placed the problem of violent revolution on the agenda again in Europe for the first time for thirty years. For the SPD the question was acute. The contrast between trade union congress and party conference in 1905, and condemnation and support for the general strike, was resolved after the revolution in Russia had receded, when the party capitulated to the trade union leaders in Mannheim in 1906. Already before that the party had accepted that its revisionist dissidents no longer fundamentally opposed the Reich's colonial policy, but only sought to 'civilize' it. Bernstein's pacifism had not prevented him from condoning the dismemberment of China, though he did not share in the chauvinism of Quessel, Noske, or Calw, let alone that of the extremists Maurenbrecher and Hildebrand. Although the party rejected imperialist colonial policy, it now found itself unable to shed these social imperialists.

Only a small group of dissidents on the 'left' of the party like Clara Zetkin (the leader of the party's women's organizations), Rosa Luxemburg (its leading theoretican), Karl Liebknecht, Georg Ledebour, and the party historian Franz Mehring, saw the dangers of accommodating to the existing state in exchange for social and political concessions. They were however unable to prevent the party voting for the defence budget shortly after Bebel had retired from participation in the party leadership; and they too were taken completely by surprise when, early in August 1914, the party and trade union leadership, the right-wing revisionists, and the scholarly 'Marxists' in the centre of the party, collapsed when faced with the world war. There were two reasons for this capitulation: fear of being outlawed – inevitable if the party had offered the least resistance – and fear of losing mass support. The Social Democrats' condoning of the war inevitably led to the death of the Second International.

Since re-establishing its unity at the party conference at Hainfeld, the development of the Austrian working-class movement did not differ in principle from that of German social democracy and the German trade unions. There were various modifications: the social and economic situation in the Reich was not the same as that in the Austrian half of the Dual Monarchy; the bureaucratic institutions of the Austrian party lagged behind those of its model; and there were differences arising from the multi-national character of the Austrian state. Although the industrialization of Austria was moving forward all the time, the actual power of the bourgeoisie remained in the hands of the Viennese bankers.

The problem of extending the franchise for the election of the Reichsrat – the Austrian parliament – was inevitably tied to the national question. For this reason, the fast growing Austrian working-class movement was preserved rather longer than was the SPD from the temptations of parliamentarism and the metamorphosis of its Marxist theory into a mere ideology for the preservation of the unity of the movement. Inspired by the First Russian Revolution, the 1905 Austrian party congress decided to force through the general franchise by threatening a mass strike and a mass demonstration. In 1907 the election laws were changed accordingly. Party theory in Austria – even that of the extreme right like Karl Renner – remained initially closer to Marxism than did that of the German revisionists round Bernstein. Renner himself, Max Adler, Rudolf Hilferding, Otto Bauer, and Gustav Eckstein all wrote scholarly works as good as anything produced by the German Marxists. With its 540,000 trade unionists and nearly 150,000 party members, with over a million voters and eighty-two parliamentary deputies, the Austrian working-class movement – despite the conflict between the Germans and the Czechs within it – appeared to be a considerable force. However, on the eve of the world war it too collapsed just like its German counterpart.

As for the French socialists, it was only through the Second International that they were able to establish a united political organization, though the tension between party and trade union was naturally not overcome even then. The decisive turn towards a re-formation of the various mutually embattled tendencies came as the result of the conflict between the neo-Bonapartism of General Boulanger and the republican bourgeoisie. Whereas the Guesdists and the Blanquists proclaimed the workers' opposition to both forms of class domination, the Possibilists and Allemanists favoured joining the republican parties in defending the institutions of the republic from Boulanger. In the interests of this alliance, they were in favour of postponing the class struggle until the successful defeat of Boulanger. In addition, there existed a small group of socialists who wanted to support Boulanger. Many workers united with them over this issue. The majority of the Paris workers and petty-bourgeoisie wanted to revenge the Communards, without realizing the danger of provoking a Bonapartist dictatorship.

In times of crisis, Bonapartist and fascist mass movements function as the saviours of the desperate petty bourgeoisie. If their leaders do not succeed in gaining power immediately, such movements disintegrate and disappear as quickly as they spring up. After Boulanger's defeat, the workers realized once again that class contradictions would have to be resolved. The Marxist Guesdists had supported the decision of the founding congress of the International to hold a demonstration in all countries on 1 May for the legal eight-hour day, a decision upheld against the opposition of the Possibilists and Allemanists. Police reprisals only stiffened the will of the French workers to participate. In 1891 all groups joined the May Day demonstrations. The government sent in troops and at one meeting ten people were killed. Paul Lafargue was prosecuted for calling the demonstration and condemned to a year's imprisonment. However, shortly afterwards he was elected to parliament. The rise of French socialism had begun. Despite its fragmentation, the number of socialist deputies increased from fifteen to fifty in 1893. Except for the five Allemanists, all united in one faction with Jules Guesde and Jean Jaurès as their spokesmen.

It was then that the Dreyfus affair broke upon republican France and shifted the conflict between the democratic republican left and the bloc of anti-semitic officers, clerical monarchists, and finance aristocracy from a political to a moral plane. The 1898 elections were held during an economic crisis which offered big opportunities for petty-bourgeois anti-semitism. It resulted in a narrow majority for the Radicals and Radical Socialists – in other words for the bourgeois democratic republicans and socialists. As a result, the army, the nationalists, anti-semites, senior clerics, and sections of the big bourgeoisie prepared a *coup d'état*. It was in these circumstances that the Socialist Millerand decided to join the Waldeck-Rousseau bourgeois cabinet. There is no doubt that this cabinet saved the republic and, by introducing secular state education, was responsible for the emergence of a new and more tolerant younger generation. However, in this same cabinet sat the murderer of the Communards, General Gallifet, as Minister of War, and although Millerand was able to push through the first social legislation in France, the government was and remained a bourgeois government. When the Châlons workers went on strike in June 1900, it too called in the army. The Right wanted to exploit the situation for its own ends and to bring down the government. They calculated that, in this situation, the socialists would also be in favour of a vote of no confidence.

There followed a redrawing of fronts in the French Labour movement. Against Millerand stood the Guesdists and their followers, the opponents of 'ministerialism', of participation in government; supporting him were the independent socialists under Jaurès. The former groups, the left, founded the Socialist Party of France, the latter, the 'ministerialists', the French Socialist Party. The syndicalist tendencies of the unions, their distrust of all purely political activity, was considerably strengthened both by the weakness of the 'ministerialists', and the conflicts among the workers' parties. In 1906, after the Amiens Charter, the Fédération nationale des bourses de travail (the National Federation of Labour) joined the General Confederation of Labour (CGT). Basing itself on George Sorel's 'myth of the general strike', invoking the mass strike as a magical formula instead of using it as one instrument among others, the Amiens Charter set out to transform the unions from being organs of workers' struggle and agitation, into being the nuclei of production and distribution after that struggle had been won.

The Amsterdam Congress of the Second International brought the two French Socialist parties together. The resulting party's new name – the French Section of the Workers' International (SFIO) – was meant to seal its commitment to internationalism. Henceforth, the French movement gained as much in outward strength as other European movements: it represented more than a million trade unionists, 90,000 party members, 1,400,000 voters, and 101 deputies. Despite this strength, when the First World War destroyed the International, the French party was as incapable of averting catastrophe as its German counterpart.

The British working class at the time of the Second International was able to rebuild a strong opposition movement. August 1889 led to the building of the Dockers' Union and to the breakthrough to the New Unionism, itself inspired by Socialists. Shortly before, Keir Hardie had founded the Scottish Socialist Party.

Furthermore, the organization of the unskilled workers made it possible to bring about an average wage rise of ten per cent within a few years, at a time when prices only rose by four per cent, thus giving the New Unionism additional authority. With the founding of the Independent Labour Party (ILP), 1893 saw the embryo of a mass labour party. Its ideology was derived largely from Christian socialist and radical democratic traditions, and it marked the beginning of the first systematic independent political activity undertaken by large sections of the working class since the defeat of Chartism. In 1894 almost a quarter of the delegates to the Trades Union Congress were members of the ILP, and the ILP began to penetrate the TUC's parliamentary committee, hitherto the lynch-pin between the unions and the Liberal Party. Although this development often met with obstruction, first because of the Fabians' identification with imperialism, and as a consequence of the Boer War, a resolution in favour of supporting working-class parties was tabled successfully at the TUC in 1898. On 27 February 1900, the first conference of the Labour Representation Committee was held and called for an independent workers' party.

In the 1906 election this forerunner of the Labour Party achieved its first significant success: thirty of its members were elected, thus breaking the traditional British two-party system.

Meanwhile, in 1904–5, the structure of the Labour Party constitution had taken shape. In exchange for being allowed to finance their political activity from the unions, the Labour MPs supported the Liberal cabinet against the Conservatives. Thanks to the collective membership of the unions, the Labour Party counted one and a half million affiliated members by 1914. However, like the majority of the European working-class parties, most of its parliamentary action succumbed to the war fever.

Ramsay MacDonald, the leader of the ILP, was replaced by Arthur Henderson as the leader of the parliamentary labour party, and on 5 August 1914 the party expressed its approval of the government's war policy. The ILP, however, maintained its opposition to the war both in parliament and outside, even when the Labour Party itself entered the coalition government in December 1916.

In Scandinavia a new wave of industrialization since the turn of the century boosted both the workers' parties and the unions. The Swedish Social Democrats were strong enough to strike for equal voting rights as early as 1902. However, these rights were only won – at least as far as the First House was concerned – after the separation of Norway and the first Russian Revolution of 1905. The Swedish Social Democrats entered the government for the first time in 1914. The country's neutrality in the First World War enabled it to achieve notable economic success, based on its export trade with the countries at war. The owners were therefore able to make concessions to the workers without endangering their own profits. Thus, after the Social Democrats re-entered the government in 1917, Sweden began to take shape as the model country of reformist socialism. Though the power of the bourgeoisie over the means of production and over the banks was never threatened, the workers enjoyed a living standard and social security only possible in the special circumstances of Scandinavia.

Danish social democracy took a similar course, while in Norway the separation of the country from Sweden in 1905 was followed by a conflict between the left and the right of the workers' party lasting for two decades. Because of the neutrality of their small countries, the Norwegian parties, like the Dutch and the Swiss social democrats, had the advantage of not having publicly to renounce the ideas of socialist internationalism and the struggle against all wars. However in the Netherlands – and only there – following an unsuccessful mass strike in 1913, an increasingly bitter dispute and split had occurred between the revolutionary Marxist intellectuals of the Social Democratic Party, Henrietta Roland-Holst, Hermann Gorter and Anton Pannekoek, and the reformist workers, leaders of the Social Democratic Workers' Party, P. J. Troelstra and W. H. Vliegen.

Meanwhile, industrialization and the intrusion of world politics had prepared the ground for a working-class movement in the

Balkans. In Bulgaria, the first Union of Socialists was in 1894. In 1903 they split – like the Dutch – into reformist 'Broad' and Marxist revolutionary 'Narrow' Social Democrats. Subsequently, the Broads accepted the war and the Narrows remained internationalist.

The Serbian Social Democratic Party was founded in 1903: both its parliamentary deputies stood firm against the war. The Rumanian Social Democrats, led by Christian Rakovsky, also withstood the temptation of trading the legalization of their organizations for support of their government's war policy.

Among the major legal parties in countries involved in the war, only the Italian Socialists joined the ILP in its anti-government stand. Undoubtedly, they benefited from the fact that Italy only entered the war after the mass hysteria of 1914 had receded. However, despite the Giolitti government's offer of electoral concessions, the Italian socialists had not only already decisively rejected the attack on Tripoli in 1911 but organized a strike to demonstrate their opposition to it. The supporters of the annexation of Tripolitania, Bissolati and Bonomi, were expelled from the party, and Treves, the vacillating chief editor of the party newspaper, *Avanti!*, was replaced. When his successor, Mussolini, defended Italy's 'revolutionary' war alongside the allies, he too was expelled from the party, which maintained its stand to the end and, with the Swiss Social Democrats, the Russian Bolsheviks and the Menshevik Internationalists, was one of the organizers of the Zimmerwald Conference.

Thanks to the theoretical work of the 'Emancipation of Labour' group, the RSDP in Russia made a quick recovery from the setbacks it had suffered at the hands of the government following the illegal founding congress of the party held in secret at Minsk in 1898. Permanently in conflict with the Social Revolutionaries (SRs), the RSDP was able to extend its influence over sections of the rising generations of students and over industrial workers. The leadership of the movement remained in the hands of the émigrés. The theory of a conspiratorial party of professional revolutionaries, as outlined by Lenin in *What is to Be Done?*, was approved at the Second Congress of the party held in Brussels and London. However, the Bolshevik faction was not always in the majority, either among the

Social Democrats in exile, or among the illegal party workers in Russia itself. When the Russo-Japanese war opened the way to the spontaneous revolution of 1905, the revolutionary role of the working class became explicit both in Russia and in Russian Poland. Its hegemony in the democratic revolution was given practical proof. For the other parties in the International too, the arguments about the future form of revolutionary activity were given a new basis. Hitherto, the revolution had tended to be a theoretical point of reference, a mere expectation. Now it became a concrete problem. However after Tsardom crushed the 1905 revolution, the Soviets – the workers' representative bodies and organizations which had arisen spontaneously from the revolution – were just as much forgotten as the debate on Trotsky's permanent revolution – the possibility, in an industrially backward country like Russia, of maintaining the revolutionary struggle for democracy until the victory of the working-class movement elsewhere, and of carrying it forward to the socialist revolution.

In 1912, as the period of reaction gradually came to an end, the split in the RSDP between Bolsheviks and Mensheviks became definitive at the Prague Conference of the Bolsheviks. The Bolsheviks came out decisively against the war in 1914, as did the majority of the Mensheviks and a minority of the SRs, though the leaders of the latter took the same course as the mass social democratic parties in the industrially developed countries.

In *Imperialism, The Highest Stage of Capitalism*, written after the outbreak of war, Lenin analysed the relations between monopoly capitalism and imperialism. In doing so, he developed the theory that the next task was to transform the imperialist war into an international proletarian socialist revolution, and that this revolution could originate in a country as underdeveloped industrially as Tsarist Russia.

We have seen that whereas the socialist parties which had not yet become large, well-established, legal mass parties remained on the whole hostile to the war, the institutionalized mass parties almost without exception submitted to their governments' war policies once the war began. This happened despite the fact that, as late as the Stuttgart Congress of the Second International in 1907, all parties had agreed to a resolution, formulated by Lenin, Martov and Rosa Luxemburg, which ran as follows:

If a war threatens to break out, it is the duty of the working classes and their parliamentary representatives in the countries involved, supported by the co-ordinating activity of the International Socialist Bureau, to exert every effort in order to prevent the outbreak of war by the means they consider most effective, which naturally vary according to the sharpening of the class struggle and the sharpening of the general political situation.

In case war should break out anywhere, it is their duty to intervene in favour of its speedy termination, and with all their powers to utilize the economic and political crisis created by the war to rouse the masses and thereby hasten the downfall of capitalist class rule.

This appeal was subsequently endorsed at a Peace Demonstration attended by all parties in the International at the end of November 1912 in Basle Cathedral. Nevertheless, when it became increasingly clear, in July 1914, that the Austrian policies towards Serbia, supported by Germany, would unleash the catastrophe, the socialist parties only grasped what was happening at the last moment. Still in mid-July 1914, there was an abstract discussion at the SFIO party conference about what steps could be taken against war in general, and not about the imminent conflict which was ignored. Only at the end of July did the European parties call for demonstrations against their governments' policies, and everywhere the masses responded. A few days, and even sometimes a few hours, later, these same masses rallied to the call of these same governments when mobilization began. In doing so they demonstrated that, in times of crisis, the militancy of the masses cannot be put on ice, but will follow any decisive lead.

Even after the outbreak of the war some hope still remained. The patriotic euphoria of the workers would inevitably be punctured by their own bitter experience. Accordingly, a party which had adhered to the Stuttgart resolution could have led the masses in a fight against its own government and against the war. However, to do this it would have to have been prepared to undergo a period of isolation, persecution and illegality, and most of the European parties were no longer capable of existing under such conditions. As a result they inevitably became instruments of the war policies of their respective governments and thereby tools of their ruling classes. Moreover, the parties continued in this role even when the masses began to stir again. From then on, the big European socialist parties only hesitantly followed the mood of their members, instead of leading them, and often they even tried, in the interest of the government, to paralyse mass consciousness and activity.

Thus August 1914 saw the collapse of the Second International. The result was that most West European social democratic parties now confronted small minorities struggling against the leadership in order to keep alive the original aims of the movement. At first it seemed immaterial whether this struggle was conducted by consistently anti-war revolutionaries, or by pacifist minorities inside or outside the big parties. The struggle only became historically effective when the masses in one of the major countries themselves demonstrated that they were no longer prepared to fight to the death on the battlefields of Europe for the greater glory of the ruling classes, merely in exchange for the few socio-economic concessions they had managed to achieve before 1914. However, such a demonstration required considerable work on the part of the international anti-war opposition.

Above all else, whether such a development took place or not would indicate whether organizations originally created to transcend capitalist society, and which had since successfully enforced decisive changes in the social position of the workers, would – in a revolutionary crisis – pursue their original aim or preserve the existing social order.

The war years saw numerous conferences of international socialists. There was the meeting of the International Socialist Women's Bureau led by Clara Zetkin in 1914, the Socialist Youth International organized by Willi Münzenberg in Spring 1915, the Zimmerwald Conference called by the Italian and Swiss Social Democratic parties in September 1915, and the Kienthal conference in April 1916. These conferences were the only effective declarations of international solidarity in a strife-torn period of political suicide, instigated by the European ruling classes and acclaimed by the power politicians at the head of the big parties and trade unions of the Second International. Nevertheless, such gatherings of small minorities constituted the first steps towards the reconstruction of the European working-class movement after this decisive crisis.

5

The Working-Class Movement between the Russian Revolution and the Victory of Fascism

Lenin's forecast that the war in Europe would increase the likelihood of revolution came true as early as 1916. The turning point in Germany was the protest against the sentencing of Karl Liebknecht, the first member of the German Reichstag to oppose the *Burgfrieden* (the fortress peace). Easter 1916 saw a rising in Dublin against British imperialism – although it was suppressed, and the most brilliant Irish workers' leader, James Connolly, shot, it marked the beginning of the armed phase of the Irish independence struggle. February 1917 saw the collapse of Tsarism. By allying with a majority of the Mensheviks and SRs, those who supported the continuation of the war and of a bourgeois republic were able to postpone the consequences of the Revolution for six months. Nevertheless, mass strikes in Germany and Austria and army mutinies in France showed that, already in Spring 1917, workers everywhere were on the move. The founding of the German Independent Social Democratic Party (USPD) and the sharpening opposition within the French SFIO and the Austrian Social Democratic Party were additional clear expressions of the change.

The October Revolution in Russia (7 November by the Western calendar) was the watershed. Drawing his lessons from the experience of the period immediately following the collapse of the Tsar, Lenin was able to overcome the tendency among broad sections of the party, including Stalin, to adjust to the ruling coalition, and succeeded in winning the majority of the workers over to his position.

Supported by the peasants who came out against the continuation of the war and for revolt in the countryside, the majority of the Congress of Soviets – Bolsheviks and Left SRS – were able to seize power. The new Soviet government proceeded to dissolve the National Assembly virtually without resistance, and to survive a struggle lasting nearly three years against the White armies and the collective intervention of the allied powers. The Soviet victory marked a victory for the theories, traditions and aspirations of the whole European working-class movement. In *State and Revolution*, written in 1917, Lenin theorized the lessons of the Russian revolution – the necessity of breaking up the old state machine and replacing it with participatory workers' democracy based on Soviets. But from the beginning the relative weakness of the Bolsheviks forced them to rely on former Tsarist bureaucrats and officers, and prevented them from fully implementing Soviet democracy. Eventually the fact that the Revolution remained limited to Russia, a backward country devastated by war, and did not spread to the fully industrialized countries, inevitably created deep contradictions between intention and reality.

Strikes in Germany and Austria in January 1918 showed that the effects of revolution were not limited to Russia. But these spontaneous actions by the German workers soon receded, especially as their organization rested on a small circle of skilled workers – the Revolutionary *Obleute* (shop stewards) in Berlin. Moreover, in Berlin members of the SPD – now called the Majority Socialists – only joined strike committees in order to break the strike. The three illegal groups of the left wing of German social democracy – Spartakus, the Lichtstrahlen (Rays of Light) group, and the Arbeiterpolitik (Workers' Politics) group – were much too weak to exercise an influence over the masses. In Austria, too, the strikers were not supported by the big working-class organizations. The workers still regarded the Social Democratic Party and the unions as their own organizations, despite the fact that politically they had not followed them for years. Thus the rekindling of the working-class movement in Central Europe constituted an important sign, but not yet the first phase, of a coming revolution.

In France the first wave of spontaneous anti-war demonstrations was followed by a new period of anti-war activity in January 1918. But in France too, the mass strike, begun in Lyons and taken up in Paris, was without real success and was ultimately defeated. Under these circumstances, the leadership of the SFIO passed to the pacifist Longuet/Cachin group, and the revolutionaries – Loriot, Rosmer and Monatte in the party, and Merrheim in the unions – found themselves isolated.

England during this period saw the spontaneous rise of the Shop Stewards' movement which however failed to gain the support of the main working-class organizations. Nevertheless there was a leftward turn in the Labour Party. The programme adopted in February 1918, *Labour and the Social Order*, declared that the party's official aim was the evolution of a socialist society by means of a carefully planned transition.

The military defeat of the Central Powers led on to the next stage of the revolutionary movement in Europe. The Austro-Hungarian Dual Monarchy collapsed. Its Slav minority rebelled. In Hungary a coalition of democratic intellectuals and Social Democrats assumed power and proclaimed a republic. The right wing of the Austrian Social Democratic Party led by Karl Renner, which aimed to preserve the Austrian Empire in modified form, was forced to submit to Otto Bauer and the Left who were in favour of the self-determination of nations. State power in Austria fell to the Social Democrats.

In Germany, the naval mutiny and the victory of the Munich workers under Kurt Eisner in November 1918 led to a workers' rising in Berlin supported by the soldiers. Despite their resistance, the Majority Socialists and the unions were forced to accept the new situation. The Council of People's Commissars – a coalition of Majority and Independent Socialists from which the extreme Left under Rosa Luxemburg and Karl Liebknecht had excluded itself, proclaimed the socialist republic. An official Socialization Commission was established to plan the public ownership of industry. However, the Majority Socialist leaders and the trade union officials did their utmost to avert the socialist consequences of revolution, which they considered would inevitably end in chaos, by forming a bloc with the established monarchical bureaucracy, the high command of the defeated army, and the industrialists. By making a radical break between themselves and the new Socialist Soviet Republic in Russia, they hoped to win favour with the victorious powers whose troops were engaged in fighting the Soviets, in order thereby to obtain better peace conditions. At first, the workers did not understand this policy. They believed the assurances of the Majority Socialist leaders and, as a result, regarded the radical left opposition, which had united late in 1918 to form the Communist Party (KPD), as merely a disruptive element. The Communists and left-wing Independent Socialists called for the permanent transfer of state power to the workers' councils which had sprung up spontaneously throughout the country. However, such a demand made no sense to the majority of the workers. All sections of the German working-class movement before 1914 – even the most radical – had imagined their democratic republic as a parliamentary democracy. The extreme left therefore remained isolated.

It was now possible for the ruling classes of Wilhemine Germany to re-establish themselves in power in partnership with the Majority Socialists. To do this they were prepared to make considerable social concessions: the eight-hour day, assistance for the unemployed, and legally recognized wage-bargaining. What was important for the ruling classes was the signing of a peace treaty which would both promote international stability and prevent what had happened in Russia. Moreover, they wanted such a treaty to be signed by a republican and Majority Socialist government. Only in this way could they whitewash their own responsibility for the war and its consequences and blame the new government for the penalties of the peace treaty. The ruling classes were therefore willing to accept the fact that Catholic workers in the Christian trade unions, a large section of the white-collar workers and minor officials, and former supporters of both the Catholic Centre and the liberal parties, all moved towards the working class, supported social reform, and incorporated it in their programmes. These groups considered that the Revolution which ended the world war was in their own interests. From the working class, apparently so powerful, they expected real leadership. However, such groups were basically unreliable and their attitude could easily be manipulated under changed political circumstances.

The alliance with the Majority Socialists enabled the ruling classes to maintain their former stronghold in the government and in the army, and to preserve their economic power. As their next move they foresaw a renewed mobilization of the middle classes against the Majority Socialists, who could then once again be excluded from power. The workers' and soldiers' councils were dismantled and the Socialization Commission was transformed into an instrument for the prevention of socialization at all costs. This led to the workers' disillusionment which varied widely in the different regions of the Reich. Immediately before the elections to the National Assembly in 1919, the USPD were forced out of the government. In Berlin, radical workers were set upon by Freikorps units – disbanded soldiers led by former army officers. This attack, in January 1919, was the turning point of the German Revolution. The murders of Rosa Luxemburg and Karl Liebknecht in January, and of Leon Jogiches in March, characterized the policy of systematic terror by which the German working class was consistently deprived of its best leaders. In the subsequent months there were mass strikes, followed by primitive military actions throughout the country. But by the time the workers had decided to implement their demands themselves instead of trusting the government, it was too late. Without time to plan a coordinated action they were attacked and defeated in one region after another. In the elections to the National Assembly the two working-class parties won almost 46 per cent of the votes. The two biggest bourgeois parties – the German Democratic Party and the Catholic Centre – had both committed themselves in their electoral manifestos to partial nationalization. In this situation, the workers felt perfectly justified in forcing through their right to participation and socialization even without the agreement of their trade union and political organizations. However, they repeatedly met with the resistance of government troops. Thus, the power struggle in Germany had already been well and truly decided by the time the Munich Soviet Republic was crushed in May 1919. This republic, originally proclaimed by the Majority Socialist workers of the Bavarian capital after the murder of the new Bavarian prime minister, the socialist Kurt Eisner, was bloodily crushed by the army acting under the authority of a Majority Socialist minister and a regional (*Land*) parliament led by the Majority Socialists.

In March 1920 a mass strike by the German workers successfully prevented a military coup in the form of the Kapp putsch; but the fact that the judiciary sided with the putschists while imposing heavy sentences on revolutionary workers made it clear where power in Germany really lay. It was therefore not surprising that the middle classes once again turned their back on democracy and reverted to siding with the rich and powerful. The Reichstag elections in June 1920 saw a shrinking of support for the working-class parties and the disappearance of all traces of socialism from the programmes of the middle-class parties. The Independent Socialists were now almost as strong as the Majority Socialists, but this proof of the political insight of a large number of German workers into the political blunders of their former leaders had no practical effect. There was a general restoration both of the power and confidence of the State bureaucracy and of the anti-socialist traditions of the middle classes. The socialist revolution in Europe forecast by Lenin had come, but had only been victorious in Russia; in all the industrial countries it was defeated. Mass strikes and the revolt of the fleet in 1919 in France forced the government to accept the eight-hour day, but the French right retained political power. In Britain, the Labour Party was at last able to break down the traditional two-party system in the elections of December 1918, and a series of strikes helped to raise the economic level of the whole working class, but there too, success in war strengthened the political power of the Conservatives. In Scandinavia, after the complete democratization of the franchise, working-class parties became the ruling parties. By virtue of their unique situation, they were able to put through a whole programme of social reforms, though not a socialist transformation of society. The Italian workers occupied the factories in Northern Italy in Summer 1920, but not even the big electoral victories of the Italian Socialists, now split into three different parties, could prevent the ruling classes from handing over political power to the Fascists in 1922.

In Finland an Independent Workers' Republic had been declared in 1918 based on a Social Democratic Party which had won an electoral majority in 1916; but after some months of fighting it was bloodily suppressed with the aid of German troops. In Hungary, a Soviet Republic had been set up in Spring 1919, headed by Social Democrats and by young communist intellectuals. It aimed externally to work with Soviet Russia to oppose the punitive Peace Treaty, and internally to break up the feudal landholdings. The peasantry was alienated by decrees nationalizing all land. With Entente backing, the Rumanian Army defeated the new Hungarian Soviet Republic and restored the feudal aristocracy. The Horthy dictatorship which resulted lasted until the end of the Second World War. In both Finland and Hungary large Social Democratic Parties and small, inexperienced communist groups had failed to emulate Bolshevik skill and determination in organizing and defending Soviet power without antagonizing the peasantry.

With French help, the Polish Army attacked the Ukraine and White Russia in April 1920. After initial success, it was defeated by the Red Army led by the young General Tukhachevsky. Against warnings from a strongly dissenting Trotsky, the Soviet Army continued the offensive after its first victories. Mistakenly equating their situation with that of Revolutionary France in 1789, the Soviets hoped to win over the Polish workers and to provoke a new period of revolutionary activity in Germany. This proved to be utopian. Arising from the ashes of the German, Russian and Austrian dynasties, Poland was once again an independent state after generations of submission. As a result, the majority of the Polish workers looked upon the troops marching on Warsaw as a Russian rather than as a socialist, revolutionary army. Thus, with French support, the Poles won a victory on the Vistula in August 1920, and additional territories with Ukrainian and White Russian populations remained in Polish hands after the Peace Treaty of 1921. Gradually the Polish working-class movement lost popularity. The revolutionary groups of the SDKPiL, of the left wing of the Polish People's Party (PPS) and of the Bund found themselves isolated and powerless in the social crisis that followed. In 1925 they eventually united to form the Polish Communist Party. The PPS itself was pushed to the right. The party to gain in importance was that of the National Democrats, the party of the chauvinist, anti-semetic petty-bourgeoisie. By 1926, the Poles faced an anti-semitic and fascist dictatorship led either by the National Democrats or by Pilsudski and his officers. Polish democracy had foundered.

The end of the Russo-Polish war marked the close of the revolutionary period that followed the First World War. While it had lasted, the working class had for the first time in history undertaken mass actions throughout the European continent in furtherance of its own socialist goals. The October Revolution had initiated this period: its victory had acted as a catalyst. However, the revolution had been defeated everywhere except in the former Tsarist empire. In the highly industrialized countries of West and Central Europe, capitalism had been repeatedly forced to democratize its political system, but it was always able to re-establish and strengthen its social institutions. Almost everywhere the working-class movement had won considerable social concessions. Most countries accepted the eight-hour day, the trade unions were in general recognized as contractual parties, and the struggle for the rights of participation was begun. Nevertheless, political power in the big industrial countries lay in the hands of parties representing the interests, at home and abroad, of the big bourgeoisie. The imperialist treaties signed in 1919 which concluded the war were hardly less severe than those imposed by Germany on Soviet Russia at Brest-Litovsk in 1918. Working-class opposition to such policies remained fruitless.

In England and France the atmosphere of victory had helped the political Right to power. The working class exercised no influence over the new republic in Germany. The SPD leaders, reformist before 1914 and pro-imperialist during the war, were even excluded from government after the elections in June 1920, their former supporters thus repaying them for their betrayal of the working-class movement. In Italy, the big landowners of the South, the industrialists of the North, the top clergy and sections of the army and the civil service made a present of political power to Mussolini whom they counted on to save them from proletarian revolution. Only in Scandinavia did the reformist working-class movement achieve real success and win a lasting influence over the state, without however in the least threatening the economic structures of capitalist society.

In 1925 the *status quo* in West and Central Europe was finally stabilized by financial aid from the USA. Here was proof that the US was the actual victor of the First World War. With its productive plant working at full capacity, its victorious allies in Europe soon became its debtors. Europe's centuries-old world dominance was finally a thing of the past. Simultaneously, the onset of the colonial revolution marked the beginning of the end of the colonial exploitation of the non-European world by the European ruling class. The revolutionary movement in Europe saved the Russian Revolution from intervention but itself suffered defeat. The inflationary crisis in Germany and the conflict among the ruling classes over war reparations did not change the situation.

The revolutionary socialist element in the European working class refused to accept this political deadlock. At the beginning of March 1919, at the invitation of the Bolshevik government, the founding congress of the Third International had taken place in Moscow. Although numerous small revolutionary groups were represented, hardly any of them were organized working-class parties with a mass basis. Only the left majority of the Norwegian Workers' party and the left wings of the Bulgarian and Finnish Social Democratic parties represented large sections of the working class in their countries. The situation was otherwise in the case of the KPD. They were only a small group, many of whom had strong syndicalist leanings, and they were hesitant about agreeing to the foundation of a Communist International as long as none of the more powerful parties were not involved. Such had been the opinion of Rosa Luxemburg and it remained that of the party's central committee. At the March founding congress, however, Hugo Eberlein was persuaded to abstain over the issue of foundation. The result was the constitution of the Communist (Third) International. Moscow was chosen as its headquarters and Zinoviev elected its first president.

Despite the expectations of the workers in the major industrial countries, of many of their leaders – members of the older Marxist Centre and of the right wing of the Zimmerwald movement – and especially of the leaders of the Russian Revolution, the fate of the revolution in Europe had already been decided by the time the

Second Congress of the International met in July 1920. Nevertheless it was widely thought that the defeat of the revolution in West Europe was temporary and not definitive. In addition, the successful implementation of social reforms appeared to justify hopes of a complete victory.

Meanwhile, the Tenth Congress of the Second International had been held in February 1919. It was characterized by the attempt to reunite the traditional Socialist parties of both the participants and non-participants of the First World War on the basis of a general understanding of the capitulation in 1914. At its Eleventh Congress, in August 1919, the Second International protested against the campaigns of intervention launched against Soviet Russia and Hungary. The fact that the leaders of the social democratic parties in the Entente countries failed to mobilize their members in active support of this protest was one of the reasons why some of the big parties – the German USPD, and the Socialist parties of Austria, Switzerland, Italy, France, Norway and Sweden – withdrew from the Second International before its next congress met in August 1920 in Geneva.

At the same time, the struggle waged between the central committee of the KPD and the syndicalists and putschists in the party led to these latter elements breaking away from the party to found the German Communist Workers' Party (KAPD) in April 1920. In his pamphlet *Left-Wing Communism – An Infantile Disorder*, Lenin supported the KPD against the KAPD and similar groups in other countries. These 'left communists' refused to take part in parliamentary elections and to work in the reformist unions. By distancing himself from this illusory radicalism, Lenin strengthened the Communist International in the eyes of the big socialist parties, by showing that it officially rejected the utopianism of some of its supporters in Western Europe. As a result, the USPD, and the Swiss, French and Italian Socialists all decided to consider joining the Communist International.

This development seemed to suggest that the revolution in Western Europe was about to experience a new upswing. The Bolsheviks now made the mistake of simply transferring their own experience, of a successful seizure of power by workers led by a disciplined party, on to the situation in the industrialized countries. They achieved a break with the opportunism and social chauvinism of the past without discovering an adequate revolutionary strategy and organization for an advanced capitalist democracy. They attributed the failures in the West to a lack of theoretical understanding, and at the Second World Congress of the Third International they called for rigorous discipline and the unconditional centralization of all communist parties. These demands were formalized in the decisions on the statutes of the International and in the Twenty-One Conditions laid down for the acceptance of new parties into it.

The Twenty-One Conditions forced those mass parties in Western Europe now eager to join the International to alter their structures. They were compelled to submit to the decisions of the International's executive committee and to break with the social pacifists or radical reformers in their leadership. The Twenty-One Conditions, contrary in general spirit to the reformist tradition of the West European working-class movement and unacceptable to its leaders, virtually constituted a challenge to split the Western parties. Nevertheless, enthusiasm for the victorious Soviet Revolution initially ran high. In October 1920, at its party conference in Halle, the German USPD voted against three of its most celebrated leaders (Hilferding, Ledebour and Dittmann) in favour of joining the new International and in December 1920 they were followed by the French SFIO which made a similar decision at Tours against the will of two of its leaders, Jean Longuet and Paul Faure. In Italy, although Serrati was able to preserve the unity of the Italian socialists at the party conference at Livorno in 1921, a minority round Antonio Gramsci and Amadeo Bordiga proved powerful enough to organize its own mass Communist Party. In the Swiss Social Democratic Party, the supporters of the Third International were considerably weaker; in the British ILP they were negligible.

By the beginning of 1921 the Communist International appeared to be a powerful force with legal mass parties in Germany, France, Italy, Norway, Bulgaria and Czechoslovakia, and with illegal or semi-legal parties in Finland and Poland, both of which enjoyed considerable working-class support. Throughout the rest of Europe the Communist International maintained followings varying in size, of which the British was the smallest. The Third International also broke decisively with the Europocentrism of the Second. Active support for all national liberation movements was mandatory for the European parties, and the formation of communist groups in the colonial and semi-colonial countries was encouraged with some success.

Despite this impact, when the KPD attempted to lead the masses in a revolutionary action in March 1921, the party's practical impotence was immediately evident. Solidarity with the Russian Revolution was not enough. The determination of the party itself was no substitute for the lack of spontaneous militancy among the workers. As a result of this putsch, which drew Lenin's condemnation, the KPD lost its most important leader, Paul Levi, who returned to the SPD via what remained of the USPD and became the leader of its left wing. The KPD made an early recovery from this setback under the new leadership of Heinrich Brandler and August Thalheimer. Due mainly to a shrewd policy of transitional demands and offers of a united front to the socialists, the KPD's influence increased during the inflation, but it nevertheless remained incapable of using the inflation crisis to provoke a real struggle for power. After the full stabilization of the capitalist economy at the beginning of 1924, and to a large extent as a result of the Communists pursuing policies based on the illusion that the same crisis was bound soon to recur, there was a swift drop in the influence of communist parties everywhere.

Inner-party democracy was maintained throughout the Communist International until the defenceless retreat by the KPD after the removal of the Communist/Left Social Democratic coalition government in Saxony and Thuringia in 1923. The various tendencies within the different communist parties were discussed openly in the party press and at party conferences without any risk to party prestige or endangering unity of action. To the industrial workers of that period, inner party conflicts were by no means a sign of decline.

The united resistance of the German and French Communists against both the French occupation of the Ruhr and Rhineland separation in 1923 testified to the sincerity of their internationalism, especially because it isolated the French Communists, confronting a strong wave of chauvinism largely condoned by the Socialists.

After the stabilization of the German mark and the strengthening of European capitalism by American credit in 1924, the left had a majority within most of the European communist parties. It was this left which characterized the Fifth World Congress of the International with its insistence that a new crisis was imminent. In order to conceal the obvious contradiction between such expectations and the corresponding tactics of the executive on the one hand, and the real movement of the workers on the other, it soon became necessary to limit freedom of opinion within the West European parties. Accordingly, they underwent a process of bureaucratic fragmentation: emphasis was transferred to relatively small factory and street cells; contact between members was restricted to small, easily manipulated groups; and instead of struggling alongside the Socialists for immediate demands, party life was reduced to waiting for a new revolutionary situation. The membership of all European parties proceeded to drop dramatically, as did that of the organizations under communist leadership united since 1921 in the Red International Trade Union. There was also a decline of the communist influence in the reformist unions. Moreover, as their own inner-party life and self-confidence waned, so the activity of the West European parties depended more and more on the aims and exigencies of Soviet foreign policy. Loyalty to the home of the Russian Revolution was transformed into the myth of the infallibility of the Soviet Union. Instead of developing an independently established, democratically discussed political strategy of their own, the West European parties stood by and waited for the revolution, blindly accepting all orders from above. Thus, one after another of the early leaders was either abused, or expelled from the movement, first as 'right-wing', then – in the following period – as 'left-wing' opportunists. In Germany, first Brandler and Thalheimer, then a year later Ruth Fischer, Arkadi Maslow, the historian Arthur Rosenberg, and the lawyer and philosopher Karl Korsch; even Clara Zetkin's influence was curbed. Höglund in Sweden, Wijnkoop in Holland, Frossard followed by Souvarine, Rosmer, Loriot and

Monatte in France, Bordiga in Italy, and Smeral and Neurath in Czechoslovakia all suffered the same fate.

Such bureaucratic 'Bolshevization' was certainly remote from the theories Lenin had once developed, both on the structure and on the formation of policy within the revolutionary proletarian party; but it corresponded to certain developments in the Soviet party which resulted from the isolation of the Russian Revolution.

The Council of People's Commissars which took over power after the October Revolution was initially a coalition of Bolsheviks and left SRs. This coalition collapsed owing to the violent disagreement over the peace treaty of Brest-Litovsk. After prolonged debate, a majority of the Bolsheviks voted in favour of signing the treaty. The left SRs decisively rejected it. The one-party state, in other words, was a product of a conflict over the strategy and tactics of the Revolution: it was not the inherent aim of Bolshevik theory. Large sections of the already small industrial proletariat left the factories to join the Red Army during the Civil War. Another section of the working class had returned to the land to participate in dividing up the estates. Vital industrial plant had been destroyed and production had sunk considerably as a result of the fighting. Furthermore, the harshness of the Civil War had produced rule by terror: all other parties were placed first under a public ban, then legally repressed. Economic policy began to show the first signs of planning; but it was planning based on scarcity and want rather than on systematic construction.

Up to the end of this period, there had been sufficient freedom in the RSDP for differing factions to exist within it. Lenin's theory of party organization had originally been conceived for a party working under conditions of strict illegality; after the Revolution the party of professional revolutionaries had been consciously transformed into a mass party. Now, after the Civil War, the main task was the systematic development of industry. The preconditions for this were the increasing centralization of state and party power (at the expense of regional autonomy), and the regimentation of the industrial worker (at the expense of workers' control of the factories and the unions). Apart from the Workers' Opposition, all groups in the party agreed with these aims. Such was the background to the dissolution of all factions in the party at its Tenth Congress in March 1921. Meanwhile, the Kronstadt revolt shortly before had shown how wide the gap between the party and masses had grown as a result of the necessary rigours of the government's economic policy.

The party hoped that the New Economic Policy (NEP) introduced in this period would attract foreign capital to participate in reconstruction. The unification of the hitherto sovereign national Soviet Republics to form the USSR, in December 1922, was designed to streamline and generally coordinate this process. However, foreign capital participation remained small. As in the period of capitalist industrialization in nineteenth-century Western Europe, the only way to raise the necessary capital for industrial reconstruction and expansion was to cut the consumption of the working population. In addition, capital investments were channelled first and foremost into primary production and heavy industry; consumer goods took second place. The result was a sharpening of the differences between the workers and the party. The possibility of democratic workers' control diminished. Soviet democracy became a camouflage for party dictatorship. Enforced economic growth through party and state administration coercion were the Soviet Russian counterparts of the barbaric use of child labour, colonial plunder and slavery in the industrialization of Western Europe.

The terror was an inevitable outcome of the conditions of the Civil War in a backward and devastated country. Its subsequent institutionalization destroyed intellectual freedom. The cultural upsurge of the revolutionary period hardened into dogma. There was a continuous promotion of education and culture, but the spirit of criticism was stifled. Inevitably, the contradiction between the party's claims to stand for socialism and the harsh realities of the immediate situation led to bitter controversy. Open discussion continued in the party as long as Lenin's authority as leader of the October Revolution was able to moderate the conflicts between the other leaders. But when he became seriously ill in May 1922 and eventually died on 24 January 1924, the party leadership began to suppress critical discussion even within its own ranks and to replace it by administrative decision. Simultaneously, there was a consolidation of the capitalist economy and of the political *status quo* in West Europe.

The Bolshevik hope that their own dilemma would soon be solved by a socialist transformation in one of the great industrial countries of Western Europe proved illusory. Nevertheless, the Russian communists at first continued to cling to this prospect and to share the illusions of the defeated wing of the Western European working class. The counterpart to this was an understandable idealization of Soviet Russia, the only country to have a victorious socialist revolution, by the revolutionary workers in Western Europe. A myth was born, and there was no critical analysis of the extent to which the forms of government developing in Soviet Russia arose from the specific circumstances of its political isolation and were perhaps not applicable to more industrially developed countries. In 1925, the Russian communists themselves recognized that the relative stabilization of capitalism in the rest of the world, and the onset of a favourable new trade cycle, would prolong this isolation. In the second edition of *Problems of Leninism*, Stalin expounded the doctrine of 'building socialism in one country', dismissing the traditional view that, although it was possible to create in Russia the political basis and the economic foundation for a socialist society, the collaboration of many industrially developed nations was necessary in order to achieve socialism. This new doctrine provided theoretical justification for the transformation of the Western European communist parties' attitude of critical solidarity with the Soviet Union into one of abstract faith in, and blind obedience to, its leaders. The inevitable result of this was that the Soviet leadership believed it had the right to use these parties above all as tools of Russian foreign policy, if necessary regardless of the interests of the workers in the industrialized capitalist countries.

Already after the Second World Congress of the Third International in 1920 the inherent contradictions of this situation assisted the consolidation of the social democratic parties and the revival of their international alliance. However, the memory of the Second International's capitulation to the imperialist war and the fact that right-wing social democrat leaders had collaborated to save capitalism made it initially impossible for many socialist parties to remain in it. So, in Vienna in February 1921, after long negotiations, these parties came together to form the International Working Union of

Socialist Parties (known as the Vienna or the Two-and-a-half International), to which belonged the socialist parties of Austria and France, as well as the German USPD.

After its Third World Congress in July 1921, the Communist International initiated the united front, designed to achieve limited common objectives in alliance with other parties. Following this the British Labour Party called for negotiations on the revival of a united International. Such moves raised a momentary hope that the three Internationals could at least reach unity in action. However, relations between the Communists and the other working-class parties deteriorated early in 1921 when the Red Army occupied Georgia, which had a Menshevik government, and after the trial of the SRs in 1922. So although there was a joint session of the executives of the three Internationals (together with the Italian socialists who did not belong to any of them) in April 1922 in Berlin, the commission it entrusted to prepare an International Workers' Conference failed because of the differences between the two Socialist and the Communist Internationals. Nevertheless, this meeting did pave the way for the federation of the Vienna and the Second Internationals to form the Labour and Socialist International in May 1923. The German USPD and SPD had already reunited at the Nuremberg Party Conference in 1922, after the wave of reactionary terror had spread from attacks on communists and left-wing politicians to include bourgeois republicans as well. The assassination of the foreign minister, Walther Rathenau, was the decisive cause of the reunification.

Ever since this period, two types of party have confronted each other in almost every European country. Each looked upon itself as the representative of the working-class movement and was united in separate international bodies – the Labour and Socialist International and the Communist International. Clearly, the decisive question of how to conquer political power – by the revolutionary construction of the dictatorship of the proletariat in the form of a soviet state, or by gaining a parliamentary majority within the bourgeois democratic state – was not yet on the agenda. Nevertheless, the division hardened and mutual distrust grew deeper. The growing elimination of the Communist parties by the Soviet Union fostered scepticism among Socialist workers. Against this background it was possible for leading right-wing social democrats to gloss over their capitulation in the First World War and give the impression that the social and political successes of the revolutionary period were their own and the defeats of the subsequent period of reaction the result of the splits caused by the communists.

As a result, during the boom period of the twenties, the social democratic parties represented the majority of the workers in the major European countries. Only in the Balkans – in Yugoslavia, Bulgaria and Greece, where the rule of law and democracy had given way to military dictatorship – did the communists have a majority of the class-conscious workers on their side. In Italy too, despite the serious tactical and strategic mistakes they had made in their fight against fascism, the communists proved more able to undertake illegal work than their socialist rivals.

European capitalism's new lease of life was buttressed by the export of capital and by loans from the United States. The enormous profits they had amassed during the First World War had enabled the American companies to modernize their means of production. In Europe too, demobilization and the inflationary crisis had accelerated the concentration and centralization of capital, as a result of which the significance of the small and independent producer had considerably decreased. The USA was now powerful enough to bring to Old Europe the production methods of the New World (the assembly line, for instance) and to begin 'rationalization'. Although New York had replaced London as the financial centre of the world, the European companies and big banks still hoped they could regain their former position. As permanent members of the advisory council of the League of Nations, did they not, asked the countries of Europe, still after all have the world in their hands since America had excluded itself? And was it not true that, after the admission of Germany to the League, the concert of European nations was being reconstituted? In addition, European countries succeeded in holding down the colonial revolution which threatened the basis of their power, and the Chinese revolution was also defeated by compromises between Northern military commanders, feudal lords and financial oligarchs. Provided the 'Old World' succeeded in modernizing its means of production, it looked as though the economic power of the USA would be paralleled by the political power of imperialist Europe.

The effect of the period of economic prosperity initially strengthened the chances of the bourgeois democratic left, which won the French elections in 1924. It also strengthened the reformist wing of the working-class movement which came to office in Britain with the Labour Party's electoral victory in 1923. The fate of this Labour government, dependent as it was on Liberal support, was to demonstrate the limitations of reformist working-class politics, with no substantive achievements to its credit save recognition of the Soviet Union. It was brought down after only ten months in office, the whole bourgeois press having whipped the country into an anti-Bolshevik frenzy. The 1924 election which followed was won by the Conservatives exploiting this hysteria, strengthened by their conscious forgery of the so-called Zinoviev Letter.

This change in the political situation in Britain showed the consequences of a social transformation which had characterized all industrial capitalist countries since the last decade of the nineteenth century and was a direct result of modern oligopoly. This transformation was accelerated by rationalization and growing state expenditure on armaments and public welfare. In relation to the numbers of those in gainful employment, the percentage of industrial workers remained steady, while that of white-collar workers in the private and public sector increased. These workers also sell their labour power, which is at the service either of capital or of a public authority under capitalist control; however, they are easier to manipulate than the industrial workers because they have no tradition of class struggle, and because they demand a higher social status than the industrial workers, a status which seems superficially justified because they have fewer industrial rights and privileges. In addition, the illusion of promotion prevents the white-collar worker from developing the natural feelings of solidarity of the industrial workers. Although these white-collar cadres perform the same function as the industrial workers in the social structure, their social psychology is completely different. In so far as they failed to recognize what their social position was, and that their interests were the same as those of the industrial workers, they tended simply to place their trust in whatever was the most powerful social force of the time. Because the Labour Party was a prisoner of its reformist ideology, it could offer no counter to the anti-socialist paroxysms of the whole bourgeois press during the Zinoviev Letter affair. The white-collar workers were thus won for the Conservatives.

The economic prosperity of the mid twenties enabled the employers to make considerable concessions in wages and social policy throughout Europe. Needless to say, such concessions were always the result of union struggles and of political pressure by the working-class parties, whose weight within the prevailing political system increased sharply when the Communist International returned to its policy of a United Front with social democratic organizations, in accordance with the Soviet leadership's recognition of the so-called 'relative stabilization' of capitalism.

During the period of comparative prosperity, the struggles for social reform waged by social democrats and communists together revived the influence of the working-class parties. This change of line in the Communist International was of course engineered from above; it did not result from free discussion among the party members below. This increased the lack of democracy in the party, and was to rebound when bureaucratic centralism no longer proved adequate for leading communist parties.

Initially, however, the workers' living standards rose and important social concessions were obtained. In Germany, the coalition government, made up of all the bourgeois parties, was forced to make concessions to the two working-class parties and to the trade unions, and it passed a law on unemployment pay and conciliatory courts for labour disputes. If it had not done any of these, the big bourgeoisie and its political parties would have lost many votes. Since the popular movement for the expropriation of the old ruling families in which, under KPD pressure, the SPD had been forced to join, the working class had once again come to represent a real political force, especially for Catholic industrial workers and employers in the Federation of Christian Unions. The rise in the workers' standard of living no more than kept step with the increase in productivity that went with technological advances. Compared with the period before the First World War, the workers' share of total production remained the same.

The German elections of 1928, held at the height of the economic boom, marked a great success for the working-class movement. Both the SPD and the KPD were able considerably to increase their votes and their numbers of deputies. For the first time for years, Germany once again had a government headed by the SPD.

The boom period saw similar developments in the other big industrial countries. After Moscow's adoption of the United Front, the British and the Soviet unions held discussions about uniting the 'Free' and the Red International unions. However, owing to the resistance of many of the reformist unions and the lukewarm attitude of the Red International Union, these talks came to nothing. Nevertheless, a permanent British–Soviet trade union committee was formed, and the campaign for higher wages was intensified. The collaboration between the two sections of the working-class movement reached its peak in the British Miners' Strike in 1926, supported by mass meetings and strikes. In May 1926, a General Strike was called by the TUC. But the British trade unions had no idea of how to run a mass General Strike and had no intention of really challenging the existing Government. There were no factory occupations, few mass meetings and only in some areas of the North East, where communist militants were active, was there any attempt to assert proletarian control of everyday social life, the distribution of food, etc. In some other areas the strikers had nothing better to do than play football with the police. The existence of the Anglo-Soviet Trade Union Committee encouraged even advanced workers to look to the TUC for leadership – though the TUC rejected money sent in solidarity by the Soviet Trade Unions. Meanwhile the Government, at the instigation of Winston Churchill, used troops to move supplies and secured control of the information media, including the BBC. Throughout the period of the strike the main leaders of the Communist Party were in jail on sedition charges. A General Strike without a concrete political aim, and confronted (as was the British) by a determined state authority, has little chance of success. The leaders of the TUC, worried at the implications of the strike, called it off after nine days even though support was growing and none of the demands had been met. To begin with the workers responded to this betrayal by coming out on strike in even larger numbers, but eventually, with no effective leadership, the strike petered out. The result was widespread wage cuts and a sharp decline in trade union membership. However, the vengeful actions of the Conservative Government and employers after the collapse of the strike led to an increase in the Labour vote in May 1929 and the formation of another minority Labour Government.

The boom occurred in a general atmosphere which saw not only a further concentration of capital and increasing power for private trusts, but also the beginning of international combines and monopolies. As a result, not only the managers of the great capitalist concerns, but also the officials of the big working-class movements deluded themselves into the belief that they were seeing the birth of an era of planned capitalism on a world scale, in which the problems of recession or even of any crisis whatsoever would not arise. This meant that trade union officials regarded the gaining of social progress by compromises with management as their only appropriate task. Because it was in their own interest to do so, it was considered that the political representatives of the management would successfully develop and balance the economy. It was therefore thought that the best way to achieve these compromises was merely by trade union officials and management reaching an understanding. It was all too quickly forgotten that the recent electoral success of the working-class parties in Germany and Great Britain resulted from a mass movement for a referendum on the expropriation of the rich, and from a General Strike respectively; in other words, from massive, if unsuccessful, social actions which had strengthened the solidarity of the workers and even won them the support of wavering voters.

The erroneous ideas about planned capitalism held by leading trade unionists were expressed most clearly in Rudolf Hilferding's speech at the 1927 SPD party congress in Kiel. The fact that built-in unemployment persisted despite the boom (just as today there is built-in employment in the USA because of automation), that there was a continuous agrarian crisis, and that small businesses were slowly but surely being squeezed out of existence – all this was considered unimportant. There thus arose an extremely contradictory situation: in both Germany and Great Britain, Europe's most important industrial countries, the two largest parties of the Second

International participated in governments which kept wages and social progress stagnant during a period of economic prosperity. One of the reasons for this anomalous situation was that they allowed their hands to be tied by bourgeois parties; the SPD by its coalition parties, and the Labour Party by the Liberals whose vote they relied on in Parliament. Secondly, both parties regarded themselves as guardians of a paternalistic and only apparently democratic tradition of public welfare, based on the passivity of the masses, ignoring the great concentrations of capitalist wealth and the ruses of the market system, and obeying bourgeois law and political science. Their actions were quite divorced from a class analysis. But precisely their illusions were the key to their power over the working masses who had voted for them; for the majority of the workers were initially prepared to place trust in them, and hoped that reformist ministers in the government would be able to obtain for them what they had up to now had to struggle for themselves. In fact, just before the Great Crash, during the metal workers' lockout in Germany in 1928, previous social advances had been reversed.

The unsuccessful tactics of the reformist working-class parties were reinforced by the Communist International which had in the meantime abandoned the United Front and was conducting an increasingly vehement polemic not only against social democratic leaders and politicians, but also against social democratic organizations and their members, branding all social democrats as 'social fascists'. Hitherto, social democratic workers had been willing to support the partial and transitional demands of the Communists, but the latter's change of line, incomprehensible to the workers, to a large extent relieved the Social Democrat leaders of such pressure from below.

The Communist about-turn came after an agreement between the German and Soviet delegations at the Ninth Plenum of the Comintern Executive in February 1928, and was adhered to consistently at the end of the following March by the Fourth Congress of the Red International of Trade Unions and, in July and August, by the Fourth Congress of the Comintern. In the unions, the slogan of unity of action was replaced by an almost openly divisive political line. The communist Revolutionary Trade Union Opposition in Germany was told that it should no longer be bound by union discipline, and where possible should begin independent strikes. The inevitable result was that it was driven out of the factories, and the Communist Party became a party of the unemployed even before the world economic crisis. Instead of slogans calling for pressure on working-class leaders, the demand was made simply to replace them, and the illusory aim was put forward of uniting the masses in a 'united front from below'.

This change of line by the Communists was based on a correct prognosis of the world economic situation. Unlike bourgeois academic economists and economic reformists throughout the world, who still believed in the never-ending continuation of the boom, Eugen Varga, the most important Marxist economist of the time, had foreseen the imminent outbreak of a serious economic crisis. However, if the Communist leaders had wanted successfully to defend the social advances which would inevitably come under attack in such a crisis, to make new transitional demands, and to defend democracy against the threat of fascism, they should have united everybody on the left. Instead, they expected the workers to rally immediately to them as long as they were sufficiently vigorous in exposing the 'betrayal' of the Social Democrats, and they withdrew their offers of a United Front with the Social Democrat party and with the unions.

The Communist 'left' turn was largely the result of the economic and social crisis in which Soviet Russia found itself with the ending of NEP, which had deepened the social divisions among the small peasants. Industrial production had only developed slowly and was not yet sufficient to provide enough machinery for the agrarian collectives to make them an attractive proposition for the peasants. The market economy in agricultural goods retained the profit motive and was still controlled by the *kulaks*; it had not yet been converted into an instrument of economic expansion. This had caused considerable discrepancies in the process of economic development, which had resulted in constant faction-building in the party leadership. The Zinoviev–Kamenev–Stalin group which had fought Trotsky had now disbanded. Stalin, the leader of the party bureaucracy, had made a temporary alliance with Bukharin and the trade union leader, Tomsky. Zinoviev and Kamenev began a new left-opposition group which subsequently allied itself with Trotsky, who had made the most realistic assessment of the situation of the West European working class. The preparation of the First Five Year Plan in 1927, the year Trotsky was expelled from the party and banished to Alma Ata, led to a conflict between Bukharin and the voluntarist group round Stalin. Stalin held fast to the illusion of an accelerated revolutionary process in the West, which would considerably ease the complex situation in the Soviet Union. From the defeat of the Chinese working-class movement, for which Stalin's over-long application of a policy of coalition with Chiang Kai-shek and the Kuomintang had been partly responsible, volatile party bureaucrats now concluded that all alliances with unreliable partners were bound to lead to catastrophic defeats. This 'left' turn in the Communist International ran parallel with an abrupt voluntaristic change in the international policies of the Soviet economy, marked by the inception of the first Five Year Plan which brought the NEP period to an end and began the intensive industrialization of Soviet Russia.

The recognition at this time by Soviet politicians that rule by bourgeois democracy was showing authoritarian tendencies was perfectly justified: but it was nonsense to interpret every anti-working-class decision taken by a bourgeois state as fascist, and to denounce social democracy *en bloc* as 'social fascist' and as the 'left support of fascism'. By adopting such an attitude, the Communists destroyed all hope of an alliance to fight the fascist threat, and opened an almost unbridgeable gap between social democrat and communist workers.

The reformists and the Communists both found themselves impotent to deal with the world economic crisis. The slump and the mass unemployment that followed it enabled the employers everywhere to mount a fierce attack on the wages and social rights of the workers. The reformist unions, with their faith in bourgeois democracy and their distrust of potentially revolutionary extra-parliamentary mass actions, were powerless, while the Communists were alienated from the factory workers because they had attacked their reformist organizations and because their abstract demands for action found no echo in reality. Moreover, the Communists had already been virtually excluded from the unions because of their splitting tactics. The Communist Parties, especially the KPD, became almost exclusively parties of the unemployed, capable of organizing demonstrations but not a real struggle for power. Because the working class was divided and appeared to have no more political strength, the middle classes, white-collar workers and civil servants throughout Europe, whose social interests the working class could have been in the position of defending, began to pin their hopes on fascism.

In Germany, hardest hit by the crisis, the coalition government led by the Social Democrats collapsed in March 1930 following the refusal by the unions to agree to the abolition of unemployment benefits. The dissolution of the democratic constitution followed under Chancellor Brüning who introduced a rigorous policy of tax increases combined with salary and wage cuts. After the September 1930 elections when the National Socialist Party won its first electoral victories, the SPD supported the Brüning cabinet in parliament and was considered jointly responsible for its failures. Only if there had been a united action for the re-establishment of democracy, the abolition of presidential dictatorship, and for a socialist-inspired economy could there have been a socialist outcome to the crisis, and the reformist leaders opposed such a course because they did not want to risk provoking mass revolutionary action. When von Papen, Brüning's successor as Chancellor, dismissed the Social Democrat government in Prussia, in flagrant violation of the constitution, the SPD did not even dare to call out its own supporters in protest.

In the many elections between 1930 and 1933 the KPD achieved one success after another. As soon as industrial workers lost their jobs, they transferred their votes to the Communists, because the KPD's pseudo-radical polemics against social democracy seemed justified. However, the fascist mass movement grew much more quickly, enjoying eager support from people who had previously voted for the bourgeois parties. Seeing in the Nazis a counter to the working-class movement, and realizing that only a belief in their party's imminent victory held the Nazis together, influential German businessmen demanded that Hitler be made Chancellor even though his party had suffered a setback in the November 1932 election. As a result, after the brief government of General von Schleicher,

Hitler was appointed Chancellor on 30 January 1933. Even then the Social Democrat leaders renounced all action and comforted themselves and their supporters by pointing to the coming elections. However, the Communists did not at first understand the significance of what had happened; in their eyes the previous presidential governments had already been fascist anyway.

The enmity between its two working-class parties had made the victory of fascism possible in the key country of Central Europe. No serious attempt was made to offer open opposition. The German working-class movement, until 1914 the model party of the Second International, had suffered ignominious defeat. A capitalist solution to the economic crisis was now possible; the door to rearmament and to the preparation of the next imperialist war stood open.

The weeks that followed saw the systematic destruction of the legal basis of the working-class movement. Otto Wels, the leader of the SPD, in his otherwise courageous speech against the Nazi enabling laws in the Reichstag, was silent about the terror against the KPD and the unconstitutional arrest of its deputies; and the trade union leadership turned its back on the SPD and urged trade unionists to celebrate May Day as a 'National Day of Labour' with the Nazis. Nevertheless, both Wels and the top trade unionists were arrested and the unions destroyed. The SPD even left the Labour and Socialist International as a protest against its criticism of the Nazi government, and on 17 May 1933 the party's parliamentary faction approved Hitler's 'Peace Resolution' in defiance of its real leaders in exile. But it was all in vain. The party was banned and its parliamentary mandates annulled.

Countless social democratic and union officials, members of the small working-class splinter groups which had grown up as a result of the sterile policies of both major parties, and officials from the KPD now began the illegal resistance to the regime. It was still some considerable time before the mass of industrial workers submitted to the Nazis, who only won 25 per cent of the votes (mainly those of the white-collar workers) in the factory council elections in 1933, and the regime never dared to publish the result of a vote of confidence in these councils held in 1934. Nevertheless, the mutual distrust between the two working-class parties continued even in the resistance, the communists still regarding even workers and intellectuals in the illegal opposition as opponents if they were from other groups. As a result of Dimitrov's bold stand in the Reichstag Fire trial, Communist prestige rose in the eyes of the other illegal groups as well as abroad, but the deep division opened up by the 'left' turn taken by the Communist International in 1928 remained. Even now, the Communist leaders still believed there was no fundamental difference between the fascist regime and the capitalist ones that had preceded it, and forecast its imminent collapse. From 1936, the government's successes in foreign policy, and in reducing mass unemployment with the beginnings of rearmament, served to isolate the illegally active section of the working class even more from the masses.

In addition, the success of the Third Reich acted as a boost to the fascist movement elsewhere in Europe. The right-wing bourgeois parties in the rest of the continent were not yet ready to make any significant concessions to German fascism; but they saw no acceptable alternative but fascism for Germany, and they hoped to steer the Reich's expansionism against the USSR. Moreover, with its concordat with the Italian and the German fascist governments in 1929 and 1933, the Vatican had shown that it was by no means fundamentally opposed to fascism, and Vatican policy influenced that of the Catholic Right throughout Europe.

However, the international working class had been aroused by the German catastrophe. The working-class movement now saw the fascist danger in all clarity and in the Communist parties there was pressure from those who did not want to see a repeat of the mistakes made in Germany.

In England, the world economic crisis had placed the Labour government, only in office since May 1929, in the position either of resorting from the very outset to traditional deflationary policies and decreasing unemployment benefits, or of adapting the policy put forward by Keynes and G. D. H. Cole, of combining coming off the gold standard with public works, protection tariffs and import controls. This latter course could have served the immediate interests of the working class and put it in a position to demand socialist solutions. In the same way, the German employers had demanded deflationary measures and a reduction of unemployment pay from the Social Democratic Chancellor Hermann Müller in 1930. Müller wanted to give in, but the party decided against him. In England, too, the Labour Government accommodated to the demands of the employers, but with opposition inside the party and the unions. Unlike his German counterpart, MacDonald did not bow to his own movement, and in August 1931 proceeded to form a coalition with the Conservatives and Liberals against it. In this situation, the differences between the Labour Party and its former leader resulted in a large Conservative majority in the new elections. The fact that the Labour Party itself had not got even a capitalist, let alone a socialist, strategy for combating the slump contributed to this defeat. But unlike the German Social Democrats in their toleration of emergency laws introduced by Brüning, the Labour Party refused to join in responsibility for the wage cuts and the decrease in unemployment pay, and fought against them both, albeit without any alternative. Under these circumstances, the decision of the ILP to dissaffiliate from the official Labour Party, however understandable, led to its own isolation and to its eventually becoming a mere sect.

Only in France and Spain did the first phase of the world economic crisis shift the political balance initially to the left. The military dictatorship of General Primo de Rivera, which had ruled Spain since 1923, collapsed at the end of February 1930 under the combined pressure of workers, intellectuals, and the middle classes. In the elections of 17 April 1931, the Republican bloc, consisting of socialist and left bourgeois parties, won such an overwelming victory that the Monarchy was abolished and was replaced by the democratic, socialist Republican Constitution of 9 December 1931 which proclaimed the strict division of Church and State. However, inadequate agrarian reforms, and the return by the anarchists and the syndicalist mass union (the CNT) to a policy of electoral abstention, enabled a coalition of Catholic and big bourgeois parties to win an electoral victory in 1933. Thanks to support by the army and by the senior clergy this government remained strong enough to crush both the movement for an autonomous Catalonia and the uprising of the Asturian Miners. Meanwhile, the military dictatorship in power in

Portugal since 1926 became Salazar's Estado Nôvo in 1933. The new Spanish government could be sure of political support from its Iberian neighbour, but it was not strong enough to suspend the democratic constitution. The Spanish workers had experienced the electoral defeat of 1933 and the failure of the uprising in 1934. They demanded from the four mutually opposed tendencies of the Spanish working-class movement – the strong Anarcho-syndicalists of the FAI and CNT, the almost as strong Social Democrats and their Union, the CGT, the small Communist Party, and the Opposition Communist Party, POUM – that they at least unite to fight the government. In addition, the resistance of the Catalan and Basque bourgeois democrats to Madrid centralism made them too into possible allies.

In France, the May 1932 elections resulted in a majority for a bloc consisting of bourgeois radical socialists and the SFIO. However, the world economic crisis and the victory of fascism elsewhere had an unsettling effect on radical governments, which found it impossible to face the economic slump. As a result, disappointed small traders, factory owners and pensioners formed fascist groups like the Croix de Feu under de la Rocque, the Jeunesses Patriotes, the royalist and anti-semitic Action Française under Charles Maurras, the Solidarité Française and the Camelots du Roi. These groups remained without a unified leadership until a financial scandal – the Stavisky affair – gave them the opportunity to mount a general attack on parliamentary democracy. The SFIO and Communist workers pressed for a united resistance to the fascists, but the Communist leaders refused, and expelled Jacques Doriot, one of the leading Communist deputies, for supporting this call.

On 6 February 1934, the fascist groups held a mass rally in Paris and attempted to force their way into parliament. The police were able to prevent the storming of the building, but Daladier resigned as prime minister the following day. His place was taken by Gaston Doumergue, the leader of the right wing of the Radicals. The threat to the republic was still very much alive and, as a result, the leadership of the Socialist union (CGT) invited the leaders of both working-class parties and of the Communist union (CGTU) to discuss a plan for a united one-day general strike. The French Communist Party took part in this meeting although it had not yet abandoned its official policy of refusing any united front with the leaders of social democratic organizations. As a result of this policy, plans for a united general strike failed once again. All parties called for such a strike but the PCF and CGTU called it for 9 February, and the SFIO and CGT for 12 February, 1934. The Communist demonstration was banned by the Doumergue government and broken up by the police. As a result, the PCF decided after all to join the action planned by the SFIO and CGT for 12 February, in which more than a million workers participated. This success strengthened the influence of those in the PCF against the party line who were in favour of co-operating with the socialists.

In Austria, the corporate-clerical wing of fascism, which had a strong military organization in the Heimwehr (Home Guard) and which benefited from the proximity of fascist Italy, used Hitler's electoral victory on 5 March 1933 to launch an attack on the democratic constitution. The influence of the Nazi wing of fascism was initially weak in Austria. On 7 March 1933 President Miklas and Dollfuss, the chancellor, suspended the Constitution. Parliament was abolished and a corporate state on the model of the 1931 Encyclical *Quadragesimo Anno* was established. Although the Linz programme of the Austrian Social Democratic party in 1927 had announced that the workers would set up a dictatorship by force if the class enemy crushed democracy, the party did not go over to the offensive. Nor could it excuse itself in Austria by pointing to a split in the working class: the Austrian Communist Party was an unimportant sect, whereas the Social Democrats had over 600,000 members and 40 per cent of the votes at the last elections, as well as their own military organization, the Schutzbund. Nevertheless, they did not dare endanger their legal status by a civil war. Their most important leader, Otto Braun, later admitted that this failure to fight was a grave error. The Social Democrat party leadership shrank from the struggle because Austria was wedged between Nazi Germany and Fascist Italy, and Dollfuss was supported by both Mussolini and the Vatican. However in March 1933, Czechoslovakia was still a democracy and, allied with France, could have come to the aid of a fighting Austrian working class.

The vacillation of the Austrian Social Democratic Party leaders allowed Dollfuss step by step to destroy the institutional basis of the Austrian working-class movement. Eventually, when the Heimwehr began systematically to disarm the Schutzbund, to depose regional governments, and to dissolve Social Democratic party organizations, the Linz Schutzbund went into action. On 11 February 1934 it attempted to defend the Linz party headquarters against a Heimwehr attack. This marked the beginning of the struggle. But it was too late: the call for a general strike fell on deaf ears. The Schutzbund fought alone, joined by the few Communists. After three days of fighting in the working-class districts of Vienna, Linz and in Steiermark, the army crushed the rising, and the victors then hanged nine Schutzbund leaders. The Austrian party leadership emigrated to Czechoslovakia. Some sections of the working-class movement fought on illegally as Revolutionary Socialists or, disappointed with the Social Democrats, joined the Communists. All demanded the united action of all working-class organizations.

The period of European working-class history which began with the successful revolution in Russia, led to the formation of revolutionary movements in other European countries, but not to victory. Although social advances were made, the working-class movement had been split. It was not really a split separating reformists from revolutionaries, since there were some revolutionaries outside the Communist parties and, in the coming period of the Popular Fronts, there were to be many reformists within them. The attitude towards the USSR was and remained the cause of this split. On the one hand were those who, without close analysis of the particular circumstances of building socialism in isolation in an industrially backward country, made a myth of the Russian Revolution and regarded the decisions of the leaders as infallible; on the other hand there were many who, also without close analysis, condemned the Revolution outright.

After the outbreak of the world economic crisis, there was a wave of fascist counter-revolution. The split in the working-class movement, which ended in mutually embittering both camps, made them defenceless against fascism, the further advance of which was clearly only going to be blocked if the two rivals would at least unite to defend democracy.

6

The Working-Class Movement
in the Period of Fascism

By the Spring of 1934 the advances of fascism seemed irresistible. Fascist regimes were in power in Germany, Italy, Portugal and Austria. Hungary, Poland, and the Balkans were governed by authoritarian regimes or military dictatorships. In Spain the right-wing clerical CEDA was becoming steadily more powerful. Even in the old bourgeois democracy, Switzerland, the younger generation of the bourgeoisie was being organized in the fascist Fronts. In England the British Union of Fascists was formed by Oswald Mosley who himself had followed Mussolini's path from being a radical socialist to becoming a fascist *duce*. In France the first onslaught from fascist organizations had been unsuccessful, but the danger to French democracy was by no means over. A second wave of fascist counter-revolutions seemed about to sweep over the whole of Europe.

Fascism was not only a threat to the working-class movement and to democracy in terms of domestic policies. Internationally, the outcome could only be war. The USSR was the declared target of the coming attack. The Soviet Union had been able to come to some arrangement with Italy, because Italy's imperialist interests were not directly oriented towards Soviet territory. On the other hand, Adolf Hitler had in *Mein Kampf* demanded the occupation of the East and the subjugation of the Slav peoples. In the summer of 1933 Alfred Hugenberg, the Minister of Finance and leader of the German National Party, had submitted a memorandum to the London World Economic Congress in an unsuccessful attempt to rouse Britain's interest in the colonization of parts of the USSR. The contract between the Third Reich and the Polish government in January 1934 showed that the German offensive was to be directed primarily against the USSR. The Third Reich, however, had by this time become not only the strongest fascist power but also the model for all fascist movements in Europe. It was therefore in the Soviet Union's interest to prevent at all costs the development of fascism in all the countries where it had not yet triumphed.

Communist workers everywhere had spontaneously expressed the desire that their party leaders should cooperate with all working-class parties. This could only be realized if the Communist International agreed. In the International, decisions were determined by the will of the CPSU, in practice, therefore, by Stalin who was now in complete control of the party.

After 1929 the social and political structure of the USSR was radically transformed. Stalin's break with Bukharin and Rykov finally led to an abrupt change of direction in Soviet agricultural policy. In the NEP period the village-community had been divided into *kulaks*, middle peasants, and small peasants. Now the whole stratum of *kulaks* was forcibly expropriated and resettled. The new policy was also an attack on the status of the middle farmers. Military pressure was used on them to force them into the collectives. By March 1930 violent methods were being used less frequently, but there were no more independent peasants, although these had formed the basis of Russian agricultural policy under the NEP. Millions of people were resettled or removed to the labour camps. Before being forcibly integrated into the co-operatives the peasants had slaughtered their stock; there was a fifty per cent decrease in the number of horses. The inevitable consequence was starvation. At a time when Stalin was still in alliance with the 'Right' and would not tolerate any measures against the big peasants, the Left Opposition led by Trotsky and, for a time, by Zinoviev and Kamenev, had demanded energetic collectivization. But what they had in mind was a systematic, gradual development of the co-operative movement; they wanted to equip the collectives with machines and to allow them tax concessions. The peasants were to be persuaded of the advantages of the cooperatives. Another old demand of the Left Opposition had related to the rate of industrialization and to the increase in production, which was to be maintained even when the pre-war levels had been easily regained. The plans for this had been drawn up by Preobrazhensky, the economic theoretician of the group. At that time Stalin and the 'right-wingers' had considered the economic burden, especially on agriculture, of financing such plans to be inordinately large and for this reason had held back the rate of industrialization. Forced collectivization had increased the potential work-force. The new collectives needed mechanization in order to combat starvation effectively. Thus the rate of industrialization was suddenly increased. With a 'leap forward' the USSR was transformed within a few years into an industrial state.

Some of the young people in the towns achieved a great deal in extremely adverse conditions because the aim of creating an advanced socialist society seemed to make the effort worthwhile. Of course, most of the workers forced into industry had been peasants until a short time before. Their energies and their hopes were abused by gigantic planning mistakes. Labour legislation was virtually transformed into a system of military subordination. A merciless regimentation was in force. The situation of the workers on starvation wages was different only in degree from the situation of internees in the labour camps.

The last vestiges of free discussion within the party and of individual rights were sacrificed to this policy. Marxism had been the product of the intellectual world of the working-class movement in capitalist industrial Europe. Lenin adapted it to the needs of the revolutionary movement in an industrially backward Russia, at a time when there was still a prospect of revolution elsewhere in Europe. But now Stalinism debased all theory to a closed system of dogma. Critical thinking was no longer tolerated. Intellectual life in the USSR, with the exception of general education, was seizing up. The revolutionary transformation of Russian society had produced political techniques and forms of government which corresponded in many details to those of fascism, or were in fact taken over from fascism. Discussion and criticism were taboo, the party and the mass-organization were controlled by means of strict command-mechanisms. The young people were organized into compulsory youth movements. Social and cultural differences could no longer be brought out into the open. The state disposed of its citizens arbitrarily. The secret police became all-powerful.

For all this, these measures did have a different meaning in the framework of the Stalinist system from that which they had in the framework of the fascist state. Under fascism they represented, ideologically, the ultimate form of national development. They were a recognized and approved means of control of one's own and of other peoples. They were the irrational culmination of irrational politics within a society that was still basically capitalist. They were not the instrument of an internal economic transformation, but of an external policy of aggression and war. Under Stalinism, however, totalitarian methods still remained, even in their most irrational and extreme form, bound to the rationality of the underlying social system, and thus to the October revolution which had created it. Moreover everything had to be justified in Marxist terms. Stalinist ideology had to deny its own reality. It had to put a gloss on the miserable position of the workers and deny the existence of coercion. Many Western European workers were taken in: the misery of mass unemployment and the low standard of living even of those who had work seemed more easy to bear in the belief in a remote socialist paradise. But this lie was not only a cynical manoeuvre to deceive people: it also showed the guilty conscience about the goal to which Stalinist 'socialism in one country' was theoretically bound.

At a time when Russian agriculture was being collectivized and the country was being industrialized at an accelerated rate, the ultra-left politics of the Comintern had been useful for the USSR. But could there be a genuine alliance with the reformist trade unions of Western Europe while workers' rights in Russia were cut to the minimum? A United Front 'from above' would have exposed their own supporters in the West to the influence of the workers in the social democratic parties who were critical of developments in the USSR. The Comintern forced the other communist parties to adopt the extremely subjectivist conception of the immediate possibility of the revolutionary dictatorship of the party. This corresponded to the domestic policies of the Soviet party. At first nobody recognized that these politics would lead the Western European parties into complete passivity and into a fatalistic expectation of a falsely prophesied future; it was bound to isolate them completely.

After the spring of 1934 the situation in the USSR changed.

Stalin's policies had demanded enormous sacrifices and had extremely important, but negative, consequences for many years. By the mid thirties actual starvation had been overcome. Some of the *kolkhozy* began to yield surpluses. Industrial output reached the same level as in the German Reich. The path to 'socialism in one country' seemed secure, if Russia was not destroyed in war. In order to avert this possibility Russia had to be ready to enter any alliance with the conservative capitalist governments of Western Europe to oppose the fascist states. In its own interests it now had to concede to the pressure from the workers in Western Europe for cooperation between all working-class parties.

So the Comintern went over to the politics of the United Front and, almost immediately after, to the politics of the Popular Front. The French Communist Party, which had only just expelled Doriot for his experiments with the United Front, now proposed joint activities to the SFIO. At first it refused to accept the counter-demand of the SFIO that both parties should cease their mutual polemics. Then on 23 June 1934 it conceded this demand. In mid July the national conference of the SFIO declared itself in favour of the pact between the two parties, signed on 27 July 1934. On 18 September 1934 the USSR joined the League of Nations, on 2 May 1935 the Franco-Russian defence alliance against Hitler was signed. From now on the French Communists were also to help in defending the bourgeois republic against Nazi Germany. In their eyes this was the same as defending socialism in Russia. These first instances of cooperation between the two working-class parties, in which the democratic bourgeois party, the radical socialists, also took part, brought the left, especially the Communists, notable successes in the local elections of May and June 1935. The trade unions were united again. The general elections in April and May of 1936 resulted in a victory for the three United Front parties. The right-wing parties were defeated, the socialists held their vote level but gained a considerable number of seats, and the Communists almost doubled their votes.

Following the electoral victory and the formation of the first Léon Blum cabinet, a spontaneous strike and factory occupation movement broke out; the workers wanted to turn their conquest at the polls into a decisive social victory. The aspirations of the workers were channelled by the trade unions into negotiations with the employers. The entrepreneurs signed the Matignon agreement on 7 June 1936. Under this, they had to accept the trade unions as wage-negotiating partners, the forty-hour week with no reduction of wages, two weeks' holiday, protection against arbitrary dismissal, and important wage increases. Parliament had to ratify the result of this struggle in the form of legislation. The Communists did not raise any specifically socialist demands. Indeed, they rejected even Léon Blum's proposal to consolidate the social and economic achievements with the nationalization of the Bank of France and the control of trade in gold. They did not want to upset the French bourgeoisie; in fact, they did not want to endanger the alliance with the USSR in any way. Here the contradictions in the attitude of the Communist Party were apparent for the first time; they were to become quite clear in the Spanish Civil War.

In Spain, too, the left had united in a Popular Front to contest the elections of 16 February 1936. Opposing them was the National Front, composed of the fascist Falange, the CEDA, the monarchists and the big landowners. All the tendencies within the working-class movement, with the exception of the anarchists, belonged to the Popular Front. Some of the syndicalist workers also participated in the elections this time. The bourgeois-democratic left republicans, like their equivalents in France, joined the electoral alliance which then defeated the National Front on 16 February. The bourgeois republicans formed a new government, tolerated and supported by the 99 socialist and 16 communist deputies. Amnesty was granted to the political prisoners from the 1934 October rising, and land reform was taken up again. In Spain, too, the Popular Front's victory in the elections led to spontaneous actions by the workers, but in this backward country the social and political confrontations took on much sharper forms than in France. Peasant revolts to impose acceleration of the land reform, and strike movements of industrial workers and agricultural workers alternated with anticlerical upheavals in the country. They were only interrupted by the counter-action of fascist and Catholic associations. A flight of capital continued at a high rate. The generals, the fascist organizations, the monarchist parties, which had been split since the Carlist wars of the 1830s, the aristocratic landowners, some of the higher ranks of the clergy, and of the big bourgeoisie, began to prepare for a military dictatorship. On 17 July 1936 the army staged a putsch against the republic, supported by the greater part of the state-apparatus, the gendarmerie and most of the judiciary.

Workers of all political tendencies closed ranks throughout the country to defend their freedom. In most of the larger towns and in many districts in the countryside they defeated the army and the gendarmerie. There they set up their own administration because the inherited administrative apparatus had collapsed. At first the workers had no arms and no military organization which could face a standing army, whereas, supported by Germany and Italy, the rebel generals were able to transport reliable troops to Spain from Morocco in order to reconquer the country from their own people. These were the Spanish foreign legion and some Moroccan units. In this situation the survival of the Spanish Republic depended completely on finding the same solidarity in the European working-class movement and among the democratic states as the Spanish generals had found in Berlin, Rome, and in the Vatican, where foreign policies were determined by the then Cardinal State Secretary, later to become Pope Pius XII.

The French workers demanded of the Popular Front government that it lift all restrictions on the export of arms to the Spanish republic. But the socialist radicals jibbed at this; they were afraid of being drawn into a war against Italy and Germany. Baldwin's Conservative government in England delivered an ultimatum on 8 August 1936: France was to continue to feel itself bound by the provisions of the Locarno agreements. The USSR also expressed itself ambiguously in response to the probability of a war which might be started by supplying arms to Spain. The French arms-supplies to the Spanish Republic were stopped. Instead, France and Britain started their 'non-intervention' policy. What this meant in fact was that the European democracies did not support the legal government of Spain, but that the massive intervention by Germany and Italy in favour of the rebel generals was tolerated more or less openly. In this way, the European Popular Front governments steadily retreated, step by step, in the face of the pressure from the fascist states. The British Conservative government wanted at all costs to prevent any serious weakening of the fascist powers; as far as it was concerned a victory for the left on the European continent was the greater evil. The Conservatives were afraid that the Popular Front Movement might become a new wave of socialist change. The French Popular Front government did not dare to go against Britain's desires. It was dominated by the thought that only co-operation with Britain made a war of revenge by the Third Reich impossible.

Supported by many socialist workers, the French Communists protested against the policy of the Popular Front government, which they had supported fully up to then. Léon Blum did try to take a stand against this policy of capitulation both in the cabinet and in the SFIO, particularly when later there was a succession of capitulations in foreign affairs. As a minister he was obliged to justify in public what really defied justification. Moreover, the dogmatic-pacifist wing in the SFIO around Paul Faure showed itself stronger than the Léon Blum group. Mutual trust within the Popular Front movement was destroyed and the government was too unstable to halt the growing inflation by means of socialist economic planning and energetic intervention in the economic structure. Thus it forced the workers into a series of strikes and completely alienated the rentiers, the petty bourgeois, and the small-scale producers. Daladier again formed an old-style coalition cabinet, composed of the radical socialists and bourgeois-conservative parties. He repealed the forty-hour week in 1938. The trade unions called for a general strike on 21 November 1938 against this attack on the gains of the Popular Front period, but their action was unsuccessful. The CGT trade union confederation shrank from five million members to two million. The workers' militancy could not be conserved bureau-cratically. It ran out when it brought no results. Certainly the Popular Front movement had been a democratic mass movement but when it was shown that it could not change society because none of the leading parties had the courage to give a lead, it inevitably collapsed.

The failure of the Popular Front in France was not only due to the 'alliance' with the Conservative government in Britain. The USSR had also hoped that it could rely on Britain to oppose Hitler's expansionist intentions. In order to avoid or postpone war for as long as possible, it had paid the price of non-intervention in Spain. Above all it had forced the Communist parties of France and Spain to restrict themselves during the Popular Front to the defence of bourgeois democratic institutions and to smaller social reforms. In both countries the party was directed to oppose unconditionally all measures which went beyond these aims and which might have led to a socialist transformation of Society. The Soviet government hoped to establish an alliance with British capitalism against Germany and Italy, although British capitalism was, of course, interested in maintaining the *status quo*. For this reason the Soviet government laid stress on demonstrating that the Communist parties in Western Europe would not meddle with the capitalist social order. The bureaucrats did not understand that such a policy was bound to weaken the Popular Front, without in any way changing Britain's attitude. It was only the Munich Agreement of 30 September 1938 which finally destroyed Stalin's dream. The Western European powers handed over Czechoslovakia to the Third Reich without consulting the USSR.

The politics of the CPSU, which were carried out by the Communist International in the Western European parties, led to another crisis which had catastrophic consequences for the Popular Front movement in all countries. The communist leaders of the older generation in the CPSU had grown up in the intellectual world of revolutionary Marxism and in the struggle for the international socialist revolution. They could no longer restrict themselves to the methods of more bureaucratic power politics; but the faction fights led to splits, and one after the other they had been excluded from the party leadership. Some were sentenced as criminals or – like Trotsky in 1929 – were deported. Many of them were, however, still entrusted with tasks in the state and in the party. The earlier leader of the right wing, Bukharin, Karl Radek, and the left-winger, Sokolnikov, were still members of the commission which drafted the new constitution of the USSR in 1935. Now, however, the group around Stalin, which had unrestricted control of the party and the state, ended this tolerance thoroughly and finally. They feared both that the Old Bolsheviks would not stand by while Western European revolutionary workers were forbidden to think for themselves, and that after the outbreak of war, now increasingly likely, and after the failure of Stalin's policies, these groups would themselves implement Trotsky's call of 1927 – a call to workers to drive out the ruling bureaucracy and its careerists and to continue the war as a revolutionary struggle, not as the war of a European power.

So the purges against all the opposition leaders began. Accusations were invented, and nobody who thought at all objectively had any doubt as to their untruth. On 1 December 1934 the party leader of Leningrad, Kirov, was murdered. The secret police had taken no steps to prevent the assassination, because they rejected Kirov's 'soft' line of drawing for support on the old opposition party leaders and members. A short time later Zinoviev and Kamenev were given prison sentences; then in August 1936 they were executed, after the first of the big trials. The murder continued up to 1938. Bukharin, Rykov, Pyatakov, Krestinsky, Sokolnikov, Tukhachevsky, thousands of middle-level functionaries and officers: a whole generation of revolutionary workers and intellectuals were shot or disappeared into the labour camps. The lunacy of this wave of terror shattered all remaining trust within the working-class movement. The Communist parties in capitalist Europe considered themselves under an obligation to defend the purges and to believe the lies which were told to justify them. The leaders of the illegal Communist parties of Germany, Hungary, and Poland, who had emigrated to Moscow were themselves among the victims. But in their isolation the communist functionaries and intellectuals who had emigrated to the bourgeois democratic countries held on desperately to their belief in the Soviet Union. Even scientists and writers of rank descended to crude Stalinist apologetics.

The Comintern was still seeking to win the confidence of reformist social democratic leaders and of bourgeois governments. Before the Moscow trials its Seventh World Congress had confirmed this course and had elected Dimitrov, the chief defendant in the Reichstag Fire trial, as General Secretary. Further, the so-called Brussels conference of the illegal KPD had declared its support for United Front politics and accepted that an alliance with the Social Democrats should be limited to re-establishing a bourgeois-democratic state with several political parties and a capitalist economic system. In 1939, shortly before the outbreak of World War II, the Berne conference of the KPD again confirmed this decision. It was announced that the only aim of an anti-fascist upheaval in Germany should be to complete the bourgeois-democratic revolution.

This turn by the Communist parties towards right-wing reformist politics seemed incredible, because in the Soviet Union bloody terror against sections of the working-class movement was at that time destroying the last vestiges of democratic freedom. Stalin's autocracy was fitted out with the halo of quasi-religious worship.

It was understandable that the distrust of the workers in the Socialist International should be growing steadily. A policy which reconciled itself with the continued existence for generations of captialism in Western Europe and wanted moreover to come to some arrangement with it in order to prevent a war against the USSR was bound to lead to terror against the Old Bolsheviks. But the Western European workers did not see this connection. Thus these politics produced their own refutation of the internal political development within the USSR. They deepened the split in the working-class movement and weakened it decisively. By mid 1938 the original energy of the Popular Front movement was spent and the working-class movement had no effective influence on any of the important West European governments.

It was above all the development of the Spanish Civil War which contributed to this. In August 1936 the Spanish workers had taken over the administration in many parts of the country and had begun a process of socialization. They expropriated the big landowners and entrepreneurs who supported the generals' rebellion. Conflicts between the members of the socialist and anarcho-syndicalist trade unions seemed to be put to one side. Largo Caballero, the leader of the left wing of the Socialist Party, supported this spontaneous movement, which nobody had organized. Prieto, the leader of the right wing of that party, and the Communists, demanded, however, that actions be strictly limited to defence of the constitution. They were afraid that otherwise the alliance with the bourgeois democrats would collapse and that the help from the bourgeois-democratic states would not be forthcoming. But the help did not come anyway, only declarations of sympathy from some sections of the press.

The legal Spanish government had been reconstituted after the beginning of the civil war and was now led by Largo Caballero. All the parties of the Popular Front, including the Communists, and representatives of the anarcho-syndicalist trade unions, belonged to this cabinet. The defence against the advancing fascist armies was at first organized by the workers' militias which were led by a few republican officers. Soon the rebel generals were supported by Italian tank units and sections of the German air force, the future Condor Legion. At this stage workers and intellectuals from all countries formed the International Brigades, in which thousands of Germans, Italians, Poles, Hungarians, Yugoslavs, Americans, British, French, former Austrian Schutzbündler, socialists and communists, fought for the Republic. The solidarity with Spanish democracy was once again the unifying bond in the working-class movement in the whole of Europe. This feeling of solidarity was strengthened by the air-raids of the Condor Legion on Guernica, the first of the terror raids in Europe in which the civilian population was the victim.

The USSR was the only state which was ready to supply arms to the republican government in Spain. In return for this it demanded abstention from socialist measures in Spain, in order not to aggravate the conflict with the British government. On account of this alone clashes with large sections of the Spanish working-class movement were inevitable. The cohesion of the Franco forces could have been undermined if Morocco, which supplied a quarter of his forces, had been proclaimed independent by the Republican Government – but again this would have alarmed the British and French as colonial powers. But most harm was done by the Soviet advisers and the representatives of its secret police who transferred the methods of Soviet purges to Spain. In Barcelona in May 1937 they suppressed the 'Trotskyist' POUM and the syndicalist workers who were in solidarity with it. Because Spain could not continue the struggle without Soviet help, a right-socialist government under Negrin replaced the government of the left-socialist Caballero. The Stalinist politics of the CPSU thus broke the élan of the Spanish working-class movement in its desperate struggle in the civil war. In spite of the courageous resistance of the Spanish republican troops and of the International Brigades, the struggle faced overwhelming odds from the time that regular German and Italian units became involved. By March 1939 the end had come. Apart from small groups of the now outlawed working-class movement and parts of the republican army, who were able to emigrate, the workers' organizations were smashed.

Only in Scandinavia could the reformist social-democratic parties finally seal the defeat of fascism in June 1934, without letting the bourgeois parties inherit their success. In Sweden the Social Democrats had been in control of the government from 1920, in Denmark from 1924, almost without interruption. In both states the world economic crisis had led to unemployment and to the formation of fascist movements among the middle class. But the incipient armaments' boom in Germany and then in the other powerful states allowed the consequences of the crisis to be more rapidly overcome than elsewhere, because of an increase in foreign trade. In 1935, at the peak of the left's influence in Western Europe, the Norwegian Workers' Party also attained a majority in parliament. Since then it has been as consistently a part of the government as the Social Democratic parties of Sweden and Denmark. The Norwegian fascist party, Quisling's Natsjonal Samling, no longer had any chance of winning much influence with its own resources. In Finland, too, the fascist Lappo movement collapsed, having as recently as 1930 forced the prohibition of the Communist Party by marching on Helsinki.

Of course, working-class successes in states which benefited by the imperialist policies of the great powers, but still remained neutral, did not mean any change in the total effect of this period in the history of the European working-class movement. The control of the non-fascist capitalist powers was once again in the hands of the bourgeois parties. These parties tried to divert Germany's and Italy's aggressive tendencies away from themselves on to the USSR and therefore made concession upon concession. In 1935 they had accepted the Italian invasion of Ethiopia, in 1938 they accepted the *Anschluss* of Austria to the Third Reich, in September 1938 they practically sacrificed Czechoslovakia, and in April 1939 they had stood by while Italy annexed Albania. Following Hitler's annexation of the rest of Czechoslovakia, they were forced into the fight by the Third Reich's imminent attack on Poland. They then offered to cooperate with the USSR, although in the resolution of the earlier conflicts they had not hesitated to violate contractual obligations and to negotiate over the heads of the Soviet Union.

After the Munich agreement there seemed to be little reason for the government of the USSR to evaluate the politics of the two groups of states in Europe (England and France, on the one hand, and Germany and Italy, on the other) as fundamentally different. It attempted to postpone the threatening, and in the longer term inevitable, war with the Third Reich for as long as possible. In 1938 the Western powers had not made the slightest allowance for the interests of bourgeois-democratic Czechoslovakia in their policies. The USSR now saw no reason to consider the interests of the Polish military dictatorship to be more important than their own need for peace, especially as the Communist Party had been persecuted there for a long time. (It was eventually prohibited and even the reformist workers' organizations were harassed by the police.)

So the German–Russian pact was signed on 23 August 1939. The confidential additional clauses promised to the USSR the areas which Poland had conquered in 1920 and where the majority of the population was not Polish. In the second agreement of 28 September 1939 the USSR gave itself a free hand in relation to the Baltic states, Finland and Bessarabia, which Rumania had annexed in 1918.

These measures were intended to delay Hitler's war against the USSR and to create the best possible starting point for the Soviet Union. None of this changed the fact that the treaty damaged the Western European working-class movement, and especially the Communist parties. The socialists and communists in the countries at war, who never ceased to call for active opposition to the Third Reich, felt themselves betrayed. The SFIO came out in support of the French government immediately after the outbreak of war, and the Labour Party had some time previously been demanding military measures against the Third Reich. The social democratic parties in most of the neutral countries endorsed their countries' neutrality. When Finland supported Hitler's invasion of the USSR in 1941, the leading group in the Finnish Social Democratic Party around Tanner actually became Hitler's active ally.

The Socialist International had thus fallen apart as the Second International had done in 1914. The Communist parties of France, England and Germany held to their policies even after the German–Russian treaty had been finalized, because they regarded Hitler as the main enemy. Thorez, the leader of the French communists, declared that the party was proud of those members who had joined the French army. Even after the Soviet invasion of Poland on 17 September 1939 an open letter from Cachin to Léon Blum on 19 September confirmed this view, albeit at the same time justifying Soviet policies. But the French communists were becoming more and more isolated and the bourgeois parties were able to ban the PCF on 26 September 1939. The last mass communist party outside the Soviet Union had now become illegal.

The USSR had committed itself with the 'Treaty of Friendship' of 28 September 1939 to a benevolent neutrality *vis-à-vis* the Third Reich. In his speech of 31 October 1939 before the Supreme Soviet, Molotov provided the ideological basis for this turn, and the cynical formulations of the treaty. He characterized the world war as a dispute between two similar imperialist coalitions. The executive committee of the Comintern adopted this thesis on 6 November 1939. The ban on the PCF had now removed the last obstacle to the ideological equation between the politics of the USSR and those of the International. From then on, the Communist parties' view of the war was identical to their view of the First World War. In the Western bourgeois democracies as well as in fascist Germany and Italy the Communists were to oppose the war by all possible means. The price of these policies was paid by the German and Austrian communists who had emigrated to the Soviet Union and who, since the purges, were considered untrustworthy: many communist émigrés were even handed over to the Nazi secret police by their Soviet counterparts.

The resulting contrast between communist and socialist working-class movements was strengthened by the Soviet Union's attack on

Finland on 19 November 1939. This preventive war was an un-
ambiguous breach of international law and an offence against the
right of peoples to self-determination. The sympathies of all
European socialist workers' parties were clearly with Finland.

Not even the invasion by the Third Reich of the neutral countries
(Denmark, Norway, Holland, Belgium, Luxemburg) and the defeat
of France brought any change in the Communist parties' line on the
war. The illegal struggle against the 'New Order' soon began in the
countries occupied by Germany and Italy and the Communists led
this opposition while keeping to the same line. However, during the
course of this resistance struggle the illegal communist organizations
became more independent of Moscow. From the beginning they
carried the main weight in the resistance. When the Germans
invaded Yugoslavia, the central committee of the Yugoslav Communist Party proclaimed an armed rising against the occupation
forces on 10 June 1941. The Western European workers, too, had
already begun to oppose the Nazi terror. In February 1941 the
Amsterdam workers struck in protest against the deportation of
Dutch Jews, and in late April 1941 there was a mass strike of miners
in the Pas de Calais. Everywhere the Communists came to play a
leading part in such actions, because the theory and structure of
their organizations were more appropriate to the conditions of strict
illegality than those of the Social Democrats, and there was a much
higher level of activity among their members. From mid 1941 the
French Communists prepared systematically, with the foundation
of the National Front, for the formation of guerrilla groups, non-
party but dominated by Communists.

The attack by the Wehrmacht on the USSR on 22 June 1941
brought an end to the distrust between the communist and socialist
workers in most European states. Social democrats and communists
regarded themselves as allies in the resistance. After the battle for
Moscow in the winter of 1941 the resistance became stronger in all
the occupied countries, and even in Germany and Italy themselves.
This first defeat inflicted on the Third Reich gave courage to people
formerly active in the labour movement. In September the exiled
leaders of the Italian Socialist and Communist parties, together with
the democratic intellectual group 'Giustizia e Liberta', formed a

joint standing committee in Toulouse, and in the autumn of 1942 they formed the committee of the National Front in Turin. On 5 March 1943 the first mass strike in Turin broke out, and quickly spread to other Italian towns.

It was the survivors of the German working-class movement who faced the most difficult situation. The fascist regime's control of society had gone furthest in Germany. Up to the outbreak of war about 225,000 Germans had been condemned for political reasons and given prison sentences totalling 600,000 years. About ninety per cent of the condemned belonged to the labour movement. In April 1939, according to Gestapo figures, almost 168,000 Germans were being detained in concentration and internment camps, 112,500 were serving prison sentences, and 27,500 were being held in custody. Most of these were political prisoners, and the vast majority were members of the labour movement.

The activity of the outlawed groups had been largely crippled by the time war broke out. Mobilization and conscription made it even more difficult to hold the resistance groups together and to maintain connections between them. With the material upswing and full employment brought about by the arms' economy, German workers were enjoying the same standard of living as before the economic crisis. Because of this, contacts between resistance groups and the majority of the population were broken. There was anything but general enthusiasm for the war at the time of the Czech trials and at the outbreak of war, but the rapid successes of the German armies in the first phase of the war changed the mood completely. The brutal exploitation of the occupied areas of Europe made for astonishingly high living standards in a war economy. The occupation forces began to taste the pleasures of being a master race. In the West the war was conducted, at least at the beginning – and with the exception of the vicious persecution of the Jews – in partial compliance with the norms of international war laid down in the Geneva Convention. In the East and in the Balkans, however, it was always a campaign which aimed at enslaving the conquered, killing off or forcibly resettling whole ethnic groups, and murdering the Jews. The indifference towards any military code or international Convention was shown most crassly in the war against the USSR: Russian prisoners of war were decimated by starvation, forced labour, or murder. Only about a million of the 5·7 million Soviet prisoners of war survived. The German population, as well as the troops, knew something of the war crimes of the Third Reich, at least to the extent that they had the exploitation of the people condemned to forced labour directly before their eyes. What would happen when the victors took revenge for the crimes committed on other nations? The air raids against the civilian population which the German Reich had begun, with attacks on Guernica, Warsaw, and Rotterdam, rebounded on Germany with indiscriminate bombing of its major cities by the British and US air forces. However, so strong was the fear of the consequences of losing the war that the air raids brought no change in the submission of the masses to Nazi dictatorship. Thus the many newly-constituted resistance groups in the working-class movement only had influence on small minorities among workers and intellectuals. They had no contacts, or only very few, with the exiled leaders of their old parties, and the contradiction between their thinking and the inert masses was too great to pose any effective threat to Nazi rule. The regime's terror apparatus smashed one group after another.

From 1943 on there were guerrilla armies in almost all the occupied countries in Europe. In the Balkans there were strong communist partisans in Albania, in Yugoslavia (the National Liberation Army under Tito), and in Greece ELAS (under the leadership of General Safaris). The two latter countries had monarchist-nationalist rivals, the Chetniks under General Mihajlović in Yugoslavia, EDES under General Zervas in Greece. The USSR tried to exercise its influence in the communist parties to effect a coalition of the communist-led guerrilla groups with the nationalist organizations, but the social and political contradictions between the two tendencies showed themselves to be insurmountable. Britain initially supported Mihajlović and the Chetniks but switched to Tito after the successful defence of Stalingrad. The USSR only supported Tito after long hesitation. In Greece the Soviet Union tried to bring about the subordination of the communist-led ELAS to the command of the British Middle East Army. It brought EAM, the coalition of republican resistance groups, to the point of participation in a coalition government formed by the King in exile in Egypt. After the withdrawal of the German troops the British High Command ordered the disarming of ELAS. A mass demonstration of nearly half a million people protesting against this measure was fired on by British troops on 3 December 1944, and civil war broke out. It was only on 12 February 1945 that the first phase came to an end with the agreement between Plastiras's government and EAM. ELAS surrendered its arms under Soviet pressure. The USSR had not supported it, not wanting to overload the war-time coalition with social and revolutionary movements in areas which it had recognized as part of a capitalist state's zone of interest.

In this last phase of the war a further conflict between the newly-awakening working-class movement and the Soviet Union was already becoming apparent. The working-class movement had been strengthened by its activity in the resistance struggle and was pursuing its own social revolutionary aims. The USSR, on the other hand, wanted at all costs to ensure the cooperation of its war-time partners in the reconstruction of the shattered Russian industry.

In Italy Mussolini had been deposed by a majority ruling in the fascist Supreme Council on 25 July 1943; the Italian upper classes wanted in this way to save themselves from the consequences of a lost war. General Badoglio took over the government, capitulated to the allies on 8 September 1943, and on 13 October 1943 declared war on the German Reich. In the unoccupied parts of Italy the two workers' parties were revived, and soon afterwards the bourgeois parties were founded. All of them participated in the Committee for National Liberation, formed on 9 September 1943, to support the new government until the final and total liberation of Italy. In the occupied regions the guerrilla rising began and, as in the rest of Europe, the working-class movement had a strong influence on it. In March 1944 there was a mass strike of one million workers in the area under German occupation. The experiences of this struggle led to an agreement on 3 June 1944 to build up united trade unions, without any divisions along political lines. From April 1944 on, all the political parties, including the Communists, participated in the government. When a general rising had finally freed the Northern towns too, the political weight shifted noticeably in the working class's favour. On 20 June 1944 a new government was formed under the left-democratic guerrilla leader Parri. The question of the future structure of Italy remained undecided. The property of firms which had supported fascism, and the feudal estates in the South were left untouched.

In France it was apparent after the landing of the allied troops on 6 June 1944 that Pétain's collaborationist government no longer had any basis among the people. The armed units of the resistance movement which had joined together during the early part of the year to form the Forces Françaises de l'Intérieure, mounted an even more determined attack after the allies' landing. General Pétain's regime collapsed where it was not supported by German troops. In Algiers a National Liberation Committee was formed after the landing in North Africa led by Generals de Gaulle and Giraud, and out of this came the provisional government of June 1944. In the occupied parts of France the national council of the Resistance retained its authority. After the Liberation, the provisional government based itself on the three parties which had developed out of the resistance movement, the Catholic Mouvement Republicain Populaire (MRP), SFIO and PCF. The industrial and the white-collar workers remembered how the bourgeoisie had collaborated and wanted at all costs to prevent a fascist renaissance. In spite of this there was no revolutionary transformation of the social structure. As in Italy, the Communists who accepted Soviet policies held the masses back from socialist action. In Italy the demands of the Socialist Party at that time were much more radical than those of the Communists; in France, the programme of the SFIO was more radical than that of the PCF. Communist party leaders considered themselves under an obligation to avoid anything which would affect the relations between the allies. And although members of the MRP and many Christian Democrats considered social-revolutionary interventions to be necessary at that time, the great authority which the Communists had won for themselves as organizers of the resistance in the war years allowed them to persuade the officials and members of such parties to adopt the Moscow line.

It was only in the countries bordering the USSR that the situation was different. Following the victory of the Third Reich a Polish exile movement had been constituted in London, based on the bourgeois parties and the Polish People's Party. Even after the outbreak of war between the German Reich and the USSR it would not surrender the regions to the East of the Curzon line which had been conquered in the 1920 Polish–Soviet war and had since then fallen to the Soviet Union – Vilna in Lithuania, and the Ukrainian regions of Galicia. This attitude can be understood psychologically if one takes account of the strength of Polish nationalism, exacerbated by the dismemberment of Poland. But no Soviet government could willingly and retrospectively condone Pilsudski's conquests after the enormous sacrifices which the people in the USSR had made during the Second World War. The Soviet Union had to ensure that Poland was ruled by a government which recognized the Curzon line as the border, so it created an alternative government to that in London and on 20 July 1944 founded the Lublin Committee. The Lublin Poles took part in joint actions with the Workers' Party which had come into being in 1942, and with the guerrilla groups in occupied Poland, led by the Workers' Party, which had taken the place of the Polish Communist Party, liquidated in 1939 by Stalin's secret police. On 1 August 1944 the Polish government in London gave orders for a rising of the Home Army in Warsaw, in order to forestall the invasion by the Red Army. Even if the USSR could summon up no sympathy for the officers of the Home Army, it was still quite inexcusable for the Soviet troops to look on from the other side of the Vistula while the German troops quelled the rising bloodily. However, at the time of the rising in the Warsaw ghetto, the Soviet Army was truly in no position to give any real help.

With the Red Army's march into Poland the decisions of the Lublin Committee on land reform were put into effect and the feudal estates were dissolved. On 1 December 1944 the Lublin Committee was transformed, with the participation of the socialist Gomulka, into a provisional government.

Developments in Bulgaria and Rumania led – with some slight modifications – to the same result. In Bulgaria, however, the strong Communist Party, together with the left wing of the Peasants' Party, formed a broader basis for the policy of energetic intervention into the social structure. The situation of the National Democratic bloc in Rumania, which was prepared to cooperate with the USSR, was at first very unstable.

In Hungary, a provisional government was formed of Communists, Social Democrats, and Republicans, after the Red Army marched into the country on 22 December 1944. Following the conquest of Budapest in February 1945 a law on land reform was passed. This destroyed the basis of the Horthy dictatorship. In August 1944 the workers and peasants of Slovakia overthrew the clerical-fascist regime, which had in fact been dependent on Hitler. The memory of the attitudes of the Western Powers in 1938 strengthened the influence and prestige, within the Czech working-class movement, of the USSR and of the Czecholovakian Communists. Past sufferings produced an anti-German nationalism which precipitated violent actions after the collapse of the German armies, and the Prague rising of 5 May 1945.

In two European states (Finland and Austria) the USSR abstained from implementing social change or from integrating the countries into their zone of influence, although the Red Army had freed them from Hitler's rule or from the rule of governments friendly to Hitler. In June 1941 Finland had taken part in the invasion of the USSR by the Third Reich. Finnish social democrats, under Tanner, had supported this campaign in order to take revenge for the USSR's war of the winter of 1939. The ruling Swedish social democrats also supported this campaign and, against their commitment to neutrality, had allowed German troops to march through their territory. The Russo–Finnish Treaty of Friendship, signed after the armistice of 3 September 1944, laid down the cession of Karelia, permission for the Soviet Union to use the military base at Porkkala, and the guarantee of legality for the Communist Party, now called the Democratic Union. The social structure and political constitution of the country remained intact.

In Austria, the re-establishment of a state independent of Germany was proclaimed two weeks after the conquest of Vienna by the Red Army on 27 April 1944. The head of government was the former leader of the right-wing Social Democrats, Karl Renner. The USSR thereby created a *fait accompli* which the other three occupation powers reluctantly accepted. At the same time, the traditional Austrian party system was revived as it had existed up to Dollfuss's *coup d'état*. No social-revolutionary measures were taken.

The USSR's policies in the areas occupied by the Red Army were not objectively contradictory to their general strategy. The Communist parties were required to limit themselves to social reforms and the re-establishment of bourgeois forms of government. This was the essential reason for the absence of revolutionary actions by the workers when fascist forms of control were removed. Obedience to the Soviet Union was a matter of course for the communist leaders. Within the Western European working-class movement, the Communist parties commanded considerable authority because they had been consistent and skilful leaders of the resistance in those parts of Europe occupied by the Nazis. This could not change the fact that developments in Poland and the Balkan countries, which the Red Army had occupied, were bound to arouse the distrust of the ruling classes in the capitalist states. When the Soviet Union failed to contain the anti-colonial revolutions in Asia after Japan's defeat, and failed to prevent the advance of the Chinese revolution, this distrust grew, although Stalin had done nothing to help the Chinese Communists.

This phase of the European working-class movement's history only finally ended with the capitulation of the German Reich. As in Italy, but to a much lesser extent, sections of the upper strata in Germany had joined forces with the Social Democrats to overthrow Hitler and end the war when, in fact, defeat was certain. They wanted thus to secure their social position and benefit from the war-time successes of the Third Reich. The attempt to broaden this alliance to take in the revolutionary sections of the working-class movement failed. The discussions between the right-wing social democrats, Julius Leber and Adolf Reichwein and the communists Anton Saefkov and Franz Jacob, ended with the arrest of all the participants and their execution by the Gestapo. The whole conspiracy in Germany was a failure because, unlike their Italian counterparts, the majority of the upper strata did not join it, but rather gambled everything on a successful end to the war. In these circumstances even the determination of individuals such as Count

Stauffenberg could not ensure the success of the conspiracy against Hitler which eventually failed on 20 July 1944.

The Second World War continued until Germany was totally occupied by the allied troops. When the German Reich capitulated on 8 and 9 May 1945, the German state apparatus was completely shattered. There was no social group in a position to develop its own strategy towards the occupation powers or even to negotiate with them. Not even the working class was capable of taking action until the return from concentration camps, prison and exile of the few leaders who had survived. The decision about Germany's further development was thus left completely – *de jure* and *de facto* – to the governments of the four powers and their occupation forces. This state of affairs inevitably became a decisive problem in Europe.

During the final phase of the Second World War the living standards of the German workers had fallen considerably, and after the end of the war they fell even further. The decline from the level attained in a developed capitalist society with high productivity to the level of primitive existence and of constant under-nutrition happened nowhere as suddenly as it did in Germany in 1945. The expulsion of the German population from Czechoslovakia and the regions beyond the Oder-Neisse line produced an enormous stream of refugees. The German workers, fully occupied with the daily struggle for existence, were for the moment unable to develop their own political strategy.

7

The Working-Class Movement
after the Second World War

The Second World War ended with an important extension of the Soviet Union's zone of influence, thanks to the victories of the Red Army, and the establishment in bordering states of governments, most of which were based on the working-class movement and were favourably disposed towards the Soviet Union. These governments began immediately to reform the social structure in their respective countries. Seen as a totality, the European working-class movement had certainly been strengthened, but its real social objectives were still far from being realized. In the Soviet Union the economic damage inflicted by the war was enormous. The most developed industrial areas, as well as the most productive agricultural areas, had for two years been under the control of Hitler's armies or had in fact been the battlefield. Large sections of the population had been killed in the military confrontations or had been murdered. The Soviet Union lost many more people in the war than any other country.

The war had, on the one hand, led to the industrialization of new regions – proof that socialist industrial organization, in spite of the primitive-bureaucratic methods of planning, was still capable of considerable achievements. On the other hand, the living standards of the Soviet peoples had fallen back to the level of the period of early accumulation; it could only be revived at the rate at which reconstruction proceeded. No other industrial country had suffered to the same extent from the war. In Germany the industrial installations had not suffered anything like as much either from the bombing or from the battles of the last months on German soil. The economic recession in the Soviet Union reactivated the barbaric methods of the extreme Stalinist period from 1930 to 1938. This applied not only to the thinking of the Soviet leadership but also to the perspectives laid down for Soviet foreign policies, and to the methods used by the Red Army in the areas it controlled. The Soviet Union hoped to be able partly to reduce the effect of the damage with indemnifications from the defeated aggressor.

Sections of the ruling classes in the USA adopted for a time the Morgenthau Plan to de-industrialize Germany and transform it into an agricultural country. On the Soviet side this led to the idea of obtaining the majority of the indemnifications by dismantling German productive plant and transferring it to Soviet territory, a policy ratified in the Potsdam Agreement. The Soviet Union still hoped, of course, to be able to carry through the reconstruction and further development of its industry with the moral and financial support of the USA. However, this was soon shown to be an illusion. The very existence of the Soviet Union as a socialist power which had opposed imperialist colonial policies and the exploitation of the under-developed countries, made it into a catalyst of the social revolution in China and of all the colonial revolutions in Asia. This process happened quite independently of actual Soviet policies; but American business, and the government dependent on it, along with the leaders in the ruling classes of the Western European states, assumed that behind all these movements was a conspiracy promoted by the USSR. A further problem was the resistance of all ruling classes to reformist socialism, which was advancing in Europe as a result of the Second World War. It was thus inevitable that American politics should become explicitly anti-Soviet and restorationist. This orientation was formulated in May 1947 in the Truman doctrine and from then on became the central theme in American politics.

In the advanced industrial countries the balance of power at first shifted completely. The liberated continental countries needed longer to find their equilibrium. Of the stronger powers, only France remained intact and was recognized formally as a great power, firstly as the fourth occupation power in Germany, and then as a permanent member of the Security Council of the United Nations. Britain had forfeited its merchant navy, its foreign exchange reserves, and a large part of its foreign assets to its most important war-time supplier, the United States, and was in addition seriously in debt to the USA. Britain was also dependent on the USA for food supplies, both for itself and for the British zone of occupation in Germany. Demands were being made on France and the Netherlands in their fight against the colonial revolution in Indo-China and Indonesia.

Against this, the United States had been able at least to overcome the effects of the depression because of the Second World War. Two events made this possible: the passing of the Lease-Lend Law on 17 March 1941, when the USA became Britain's supplier, and then, the Japanese attack on Pearl Harbor and Germany's declaration of war in December 1941, when the United States became one of the warring nations. Beyond this the USA was able to modernize and expand its industry at a time when the industrially developed capitalist states in Europe were, with the exception of Britain, being exploited by the Third Reich, and the recently developed Soviet industry had been largely destroyed by the German occupation. The USA had risen to being the dominant creditor of all the other capitalist states. War-time contracts made it possible for the US government to promote scientific and technical research, the development of atomic research and eventually the production of the atom bomb. The basis for a further increase in productivity through automation and the harnessing of atomic energy was thus created. It only required the results of the research to be made available to industry. With the dropping of the atom bombs on Hiroshima and Nagasaki in August 1945 the USA had given clear proof of its military power, so that its leading position in the world seemed indisputable. At the same time, the USA had made it known that it was ready to apply this power quite indiscriminately without humanitarian considerations or any reference to international law. The assumption that the Soviet Union was not going to be in a position to produce equivalent arms for a very long time intensified the American policy of confrontation. This was soon no longer oriented towards containment but towards the 'roll-back' of the USSR and of every socialist, communist and colonial-revolutionary movement in the world. An aspect of these policies was the systematization of a politically determined plan for the export of capital with the proclamation of the Marshall Plan in July 1947. The Marshall

Plan furnished the initial impetus for rebuilding the European economy, but it was only accepted at the cost of abstaining from socialist policies.

Such was the background to the reconstruction and the policies of the trade union and political organizations of the working class in the European countries after the end of the war. They had more or less to fit into it, being too weak to play a determining role. This context also had an important influence on their ideological development.

The British Labour Party had entered Churchill's cabinet in 1940 after the defeat of France and Chamberlain's fall. With the support of some liberal intellectuals, the coalition Government had introduced social reforms. The outline of a paternalistic welfare state was laid down in the Beveridge Report, and education reform was started with the 1944 Education Bill introduced by the Conservative Minister, Butler. The Labour Party did not wish to continue the coalition after the war and won a resounding victory in the General Election of 5 July 1945. With a total of twelve million votes it had gained 3·5 million votes over the last election in 1935, and for the first time in its history it now had an absolute majority in parliament. The possibility for a parliamentary transition to socialism seemed propitious. There was widespread mass enthusiasm for socialist ideas: the memory of depression and appeasement in the thirties had discredited much of bourgeois politics, while the war had furnished a direct experience of the advantages of planning and stimulated the political awareness and expectations of the masses. The delegates to the Labour Party Conference before the election imposed a radical programme of nationalization upon the generally timid Labour leadership. Although the economic situation prevailing in the country severely restricted its freedom of action, the new Labour government did inherit the war-time instruments of economic planning and the more equal distribution of economic resources which war-time shortages had made necessary. Moreover the experience of war had at last taught the governments of capitalist countries how to avoid mass unemployment. In the event the Labour government was able for a time to conserve war-time gains and to enact significant new reforms. Of these the most important was undoubtedly the National

Health Service fought through by the Health Minister, Aneurin Bevan, against noisy opposition from the medical establishment and the bourgeois parties. The bankrupt coal-mining industry and railways were nationalized, as were the Bank of England and later the iron and steel industry. In all cases the former owners were generously compensated and the capitalist management structure was retained. For the leaders of the Labour Party and the Trade Unions there was no question of really expropriating the great concentrations of private wealth. They were quite satisfied to achieve what social reforms were possible so long as they could be handed down to the workers from parliament. The great capitalist interests which thus survived were able to outlive the reformist measures of the Labour government, and generate anew economic inequalities at the pre-war level. In the fifties the proportion of working-class children at university was no higher than it had been before the war and the net effect of the other reformist measures was to redistribute resources *within* rather than *between* the social classes. Even during the Labour administration the scope for reformist measures was limited by the difficult economic situation and the growing pressures of the Cold War. The government was unable to lift the rationing of food and most consumer goods, and because of this it lost the support of the middle classes. It did not dare to arouse the enthusiasm of the workers for directly revolutionary policies which could have carried along the white-collar workers. Britain under Labour helped to pioneer the transition from colonial to neo-colonial domination. On 15 August 1947 India, Pakistan and Ceylon were given political independence. However, the Labour government preserved the economic heart of British imperialism (oil in the Middle East, rubber plantations in Malaya, gold in South Africa) and where necessary they defended it by force of arms.

External pressure from the USA and the economic situation in Britain itself led to its gradual loss of independence, first in its policies towards Germany, then in its policies towards Eastern Europe. Due to US pressure, the same Labour government which had nationalized coal, iron, and steel production in Britain had to forbid the North Rhine-Westphalian parliament from taking measures to nationalize sectors of industry, something which had been demanded by the employee wing of even the German Christian Democratic Union, as well as by both working-class parties. The plans of the socialist director of the Economic Office of the British zone, Dr Victor Agartz, also fell victim to the subordination of the zone to the American *diktat* in 'bi-zonal' affairs. Soon Britain was obliged to cooperate in American military moves against the Soviet Union, to join the Brussels pact, and to increase arms' expenditure. There then followed agreement on the final partition of Germany as proposed by the USA, with the foundation of a West German state at the London Conference in February 1948. In excluding the Soviet Union, this Conference clearly contravened the Potsdam Agreement and the arrangements made between the four occupation powers. On 4 April 1949 England joined NATO. The Foreign Minister rationalized this change of direction as a 'resolute acceptance of American leadership'. The doubtful value of this ideology was made clear by Portugal's founder-membership of the Treaty which, according to its preamble, was meant to serve 'the defence of the foundations of democracy'.

In the 1950 elections the Labour Party was still able to increase its vote to 13·3 million against the Conservatives' 12·4 million. However, the arithmetics of the British electoral system of the straight majority meant that the Labour Party's majority of seats shrank to five. Aneurin Bevan and Harold Wilson soon saw reason openly to oppose continued full-scale rearmament because it endangered the financing of progressive social policy. Warning against policies which made the Labour Party an American ally and an opponent of the Asian revolutions, they resigned from the government. In the 1951 elections that followed soon after, the Labour Party lost its parliamentary majority. The working class was thus deposed for over a decade from the political leadership of the only Western European power on which it had been able to exercise influence in the post-war period. The Labour Party was not removed from power in the 1951 elections because it had lost its voters; its share of the votes had, on the contrary, risen from 47·8 per cent in 1945 to 48·8 per cent. But the effect of the straight majority vote with single-seat constituencies, and of the constituency boundaries, was to favour the independent middle class and the upper strata of employees at the expense of the industrial workers who live in high-density areas. Thus, although Labour had a majority of votes over the Conservatives, they actually had a minority of seats.

The return of the representatives of private property into government office led to the denationalization of the iron and steel industry. The unprofitable coal mines were however left in the hands of the state. The socialization of losses is as easily reconciled with the ideology of the 'free market economy' as with the maintenance of the late capitalist economic structure. However, even the Conservatives did not infringe the progress made in social policy enacted between 1945 and 1951. The upward swing which then followed in the whole capitalist world, with the USA's return to full-scale rearmament, stabilized Conservative domination for two further electoral periods.

But the investment policy of British monopoly capital did not build on the high profits of the late forties and early fifties in order to modernize and rationalize British industry. The dominance of the financial oligarchy of the City of London forced British governments to defend the international role of the pound sterling even when this conflicted with the interests of the industrial sector. Successive freezes were imposed on the economy to avert the prospect of devaluation. At the same time British financial interests found a higher rate of return abroad and there was a renewed export of capital – most of it to the areas where Britain retained political influence or shared it with the senior imperialist partner, the United States. When the Labour Party won the elections of 15 October 1964 it inherited the management of a capitalist economy plagued by stagnation and crisis.

Between 1951 and 1964 there were considerable changes within the British working-class movement. The Labour left led by Bevan had constituted an opposition group in the years after 1951, insisting that the goal of nationalization should be maintained for the key sections of the economy; in foreign policy they called for détente with the USSR and opposed the repression of colonial revolts. But by the late fifties and early sixties the focus of the left had switched from the Bevanite group in parliament to the development of the movement outside. The Campaign for Nuclear Disarmament, which mobilized thousands of young people against the politics of the Cold

War, found support within the trade unions and for one brief year carried a majority at the Labour Party Conference in 1960. Since at least the time of the General Strike, the Trade Unions had usually been on the right of the Labour Party using their block votes to support the policies of leaders like Ramsay MacDonald and Clement Attlee. Now there was some sign of a radicalization in the unions. The full-employment conditions of this period encouraged the development of militant local struggles for better wages and conditions; shop stewards emerged in each factory as the direct representatives of the workers in these struggles. The national leadership of the Transport and General Workers' Union, and later of the Amalgamated Engineering Federation, the two largest unions, came partially to reflect this re-emergence of economic militancy. After Bevan's death and after Wilson had succeeded Hugh Gaitskell as leader of the Labour Party in 1961, the leadership of the left was to be found in the Trade Unions and not the Labour Party. The links of the Labour Party with the working class had always mainly derived from the unions and the period after 1951 saw a notable decline in the direct participation of workers in the party itself. It also saw the emergence of a coherent right-wing ideology within the Labour Party which the left was quite unable to match – because of the Party's uninspiring record many of the thinkers of the new left currents were not to be found within it. The professional Labour politicians believed that stable majorities and a lasting partnership with industrial management could only be won by accommodating to the middle class and defending the privileges of the Western industrial powers. The transformation of a party of the working class into a permanently governing 'popular party' meant that this group considered it desirable to abandon even the theoretical goal of a socialist society and to give practical support to the containment of industrial struggle and the repression of national liberation movements. Although the right wing was unsuccessful in a move to take out any reference to public ownership in the Party's statement of aims, their ideas came to dominate the Parliamentary Labour Party. Harold Wilson, who had earlier posed as a man of the left, succeeded in giving this ideology a more dynamic and demagogic twist which helped the Labour Party win the 1964 General Election. He claimed that a Labour Government under his leadership would modernize the archaic structures of the British economy and that the 'white heat of the technological revolution' would dissolve capitalism without the workers having to do anything directly about it themselves.

The attempt made by the United States to isolate the Soviet Union and to narrow its zone of influence by a combination of politically directed economic aid to the European capitalist powers and military pressure had made imperative an accelerated rebuilding of Soviet society after 1945, and the consolidation of Soviet control of Eastern Europe. This meant the socialization of the means of industrial production and the collectivization of agricultural production by bureaucratic-dictatorial means. The Soviet Union attempted to give these policies a sound basis by reorganizing and restructuring the working-class parties. In 1948 the socialist parties in Rumania, Bulgaria, Hungary, Czechoslovakia, and Poland, were united one after the other, following the neutralization of the right-wing groups in the leadership. In all these cases the leadership of the united parties fell to those Communists who were ready to use Stalinist methods of control both within the party and in relation to the working class and the rest of the population. The Communist leaders who resisted like Gomulka were replaced by Stalinists. Leaders of the anti-fascist groups, which had earlier fought alongside the socialist organizations and had then cooperated in the reconstruction were removed from the organizations which then became more or less unconscious instruments of Soviet policy. Nor was it always necessary for the Red Army to be present in order to carry out the reorganization of the working-class movement and to introduce the Stalinist forms of control which gave birth to the 'Popular Democracies'. In Czechoslovakia in the more or less free elections of May 1945, the Communist Party had received 38 per cent and the Social Democrats almost 14 per cent of the votes. So the Communists controlled the government coalition, being by far the strongest party. When the bourgeois parties left the cabinet in February 1948, worried at the course of events and suspicious of the activities of the Communist Minister of the Interior, the Communists answered by mobilizing their supporters in the factories and in the trade union confederation. The left Social Democrats supported them. The decision was thus made in favour of the Communists without there being Soviet troops in the country. But the Communist leadership which had effected this transformation and enjoyed genuine popular support was soon to be purged by Stalin.

In September 1947 the Communist Information Office (Cominform) was founded in Warsaw. Its purpose was to mediate the ideological influence of the CPSU, and to give support to Soviet hegemony. Apart from the Communist parties of the Eastern European countries mentioned, the Yugoslav, French, Italian and other European parties also belonged to Cominform. In 1948 Tito, the Yugoslav partisan leader, challenged Stalin's blatant attempts to impose Soviet domination on Yugoslavia and was promptly branded as a fascist. The Yugoslav Party was expelled from the Cominform. Soviet control tightened throughout Eastern Europe because there existed groups within the governments and Communist leaderships favourable to Tito.

The Stalinization of the parties and of the forms of control in the so-called satellite states proceeded apace – from 1949 on they were economically integrated into the council for mutual economic aid (Comecon), and from 1955 on militarily and politically integrated into the system of the Warsaw pact. Communist leaders whose views deviated from Stalin's 'line' were condemned on the basis of invented accusations as in the Russian show trials of 1936–8 – leaders like Rajk in Budapest in September 1949, Kostov in Sofia in December 1949, and Slansky and Clementis in Prague in 1952. Gomulka, Kadar and Husak, in Poland, Hungary and Czechoslovakia respectively, survived but were held in prison for years. In 1956, after the Twentieth Party Congress of the CPSU, the party leaders admitted these trials had been faked and began to rehabilitate some of the victims.

The economies of these countries had to produce the means of investment necessary for accelerated industrialization. More than this, they were still largely tuned to the needs of the USSR. In countries like Czechoslovakia, Hungary, and in part Poland, which were already relatively highly industrialized, this meant the living standard of the working masses stagnated and only slowly rose above the lowest level of the world economic crisis and the occupation. At the same time, however, the workers in the neighbouring capitalist countries were able to improve their living conditions considerably by means of trade union struggles; productivity rose in the long period of high economic activity which began with the Korean crisis and full-scale rearmament. The Stalinists thus considered it necessary to prohibit both all personal relations with the Western countries, and the free circulation of information. The workers over whom the bureaucrats exercised control were as far as possible deprived of knowledge of the situation. The purpose of this 'iron curtain' was only fulfilled to a certain degree. Certainly the workers in the Eastern states attained social rights which went well beyond those of the working class in the capitalist states, and, above all, they had gained an educational system without social barriers. However, the system of economic planning remained completely bureaucratic; it did not allow them any self-management or trade union independence. The workers could recognize the partly avoidable planning mistakes, but not the objective of the planning. Thus the gap between the Communist Parties and the working masses steadily widened.

When the Soviet Union had completed its reconstruction and had gone further to become the second industrial power in the world, the situation was somewhat relaxed, with a crisis in the methods and internal regime of the CPSU. The Soviet Union's leap forward after 1945 was of the same order as that made after 1929. The ruling strata in the capitalist states had at that time not believed the change possible, and again at the height of the Cold War they did not recognize the new change. Only when the first satellite was launched in 1957 and the second reached the moon on 14 September 1959 did people in the old industrial countries start to realize to what extent the productive and military capacity of the Soviet economy had grown. The Cuban revolution in 1959 and 1960 underlined this fact. Although the Soviet-oriented Communist Party had not led the revolution, Soviet economic and military assistance was vital in Fidel Castro's confrontation with the United States.

Russia's forced industrialization by the wasteful methods of a brutal bureaucracy had accompanied the development of Stalin's autocracy. By the time he died in March 1953, the productivity of the Soviet economy had increased to such an extent that by any reckoning Stalin's rule had become an odious anachronism. The political conflicts which followed were decided at the very top of the Party but without recourse to administrative terror and show trials. Many of the labour camps, where some ten million Soviet citizens had slaved in appalling conditions, were closed down after revolts in Vorkuta and other areas. In 1956 at the Twentieth Congress of the CPSU, Nikita Khrushchev, the new First Secretary, delivered a secret speech which attacked Stalin and sought to initiate a re-evaluation of the period of the 'cult of personality'. Khrushchev denounced many of the purges and show trials as fraudulent, especially where they concerned former Stalinists like himself, and also exposed Stalin's military bungling at the beginning of the war. In 1957 the Central Committee voted against the so-called anti-Party group which had taken fright at the process of de-Stalinization. However, although intellectual life was considerably relaxed and the arbitrary power of the secret police was curbed, the underlying political structure established by Stalin was preserved. There was no free political debate even within the party and all public institutions, including the unions, were used to control the workers. A secretive top bureaucratic group in control of the Party continued to monop-olize not only all power but also all political discussion. Liberalization of the economy rather than democratization of political life was promoted. An attempt was made to restructure the relation between consumer and producer by means of market type mechanisms. Agriculture, which still suffered from the effects of Stalin's collectiv-ization policies, retarded the growth of the whole economy. Bureau-cratic incompetence continued to produce shortages of staple consumer goods and thus belied the promises of plenty contained in the 1961 Party programme. However, despite his hesitations, Khrushchev had sought a political reckoning with the past and probably wished to further modify the Stalinist system of controls. On 17 October 1964 he was deposed by the Central Committee. Setbacks in economic policy (agriculture) and foreign policy (the unsuccessful attempt to install missiles in Cuba in late 1962) contri-buted to his fall but so too did a fear of further experiments in de-Stalinization. From this time on there was a slow but steady retreat from Khrushchev's attempts at controlled liberalization. However there could be no full-scale return to the Stalin period: the

Party bureaucracy could no longer whip itself into such a terroristic fanaticism.

The crisis of bureaucratic control over Soviet society after Stalin's death was bound to find its reflection in the relations between the USSR and the system of states bound to it, and in particular the relations between the CPSU and the parties in those countries. In April 1955 the Cominform was dissolved; the communist parties outside the Soviet Union were to be granted greater independence. This relaxation of control led to mass actions by workers and young intellectuals in Poland and in Hungary. Poland experienced mass strikes in Poznan in June 1956. The central committee of the Unified Workers' Party rehabilitated Gomulka and his supporters, but left the former Stalinists at the head of the party, particularly the Minister for Defence and the one-time Soviet Marshal, Rokossovsky. The protests by workers and intellectuals continued unabated. They were directed not against the socialist economic system, but against its Stalinist form and methods of control in the state and in the party. Thus the Central Committee was forced entirely to reconstitute the party leadership, and thereby also the political leadership of the state, in its session of 19–21 October. After negotiations with a delegation from the central committee of the CPSU, of which Khrushchev, Kaganovitch, Molotov and Mikoyan were members, almost complete control was handed over to Gomulka and his group, but other currents were also represented in the central committee and in the politburo. The collectivization of agriculture which had in any case not been very successful was largely halted, and intellectual life was liberalized. As before, the comparatively strong bourgeois groups in Poland, and the influence of the Catholic church on large sections of the population, made it necessary for the government to manoeuvre with care if the reformed party was still to retain control over society. The contradictions between different groupings within the party leadership remained. In this complicated situation a liberalization of society was bound to remain within limits. However, for a time Polish Marxism was freed from many of its old fetters; its contributions to philosophy, law, and economics attained European status with the works of Leszek Kolakowski, Adam Schaff and Oskar Lange.

In Hungary, after the rehabilitation of the defendants in the Rajk-trial in July 1956, Mátyas Rákósi, the representative of extreme Stalinism, was forced to resign. The Petöfy-circle, an association of communist writers and intellectuals, became the centre of opposition against what remained of Stalinism. By October the tensions came to a climax: in the days following 21 October student demonstrations against the party leaders took place, and on 23 October there was a mass demonstration in Budapest in which many industrial workers took part. Imre Nagy, Kadar, and Munnich, who had all been rehabilitated, along with the renowned Marxist philosopher and literary critic, Georg Lukács, were coopted into the party leadership. The demonstrations turned into a rising. Gerö alerted the Soviet troops; Imre Nagy was appointed Premier, and Kadar was appointed party secretary in place of Gerö; the Soviet troops were withdrawn from Budapest again. The party and the state apparatus had collapsed and workers' councils were set up in Budapest. A general witch-hunt against former Stalinist police officials started and several were lynched. Imre Nagy tried to calm the excited masses by giving notice of Hungary's intention to quit the Warsaw pact, proclaiming Hungary's neutrality between the two blocs. Kadar negotiated with the Soviet troops and with Soviet backing formed a new party and a counter-government which was installed by the intervention of the Red Army on 4 November 1956.

The Kadar government was furnished with considerable economic aid by the Soviet Union. By the mid sixties it had achieved one of the higher standards of living in Eastern Europe and permitted a certain relaxation of bureaucratic control.

In the other 'people's democracies' and in their respective communist parties, the new course was introduced slowly by means of party leaders' decisions mediated through more or less bureaucratic channels. There was no intervention from the masses and no abrupt change in the leadership. In Bulgaria de-Stalinization began later and the dependence of the party leadership on the CPSU was therefore considerably greater than elsewhere. In Rumania the dispute between the Soviet Union and China in the sixties led to a breakthrough to independent politics. This contradiction between the giant communist powers reflected definite differences of national interest but it was also a reflection of different histories and levels of development.

As an established industrial power with its own, albeit small, sphere of influence, and only a distant memory of revolution, the Soviet Union wished to come to some agreement with the United States. The Chinese leaders were deeply suspicious of the Russian advocacy of 'peaceful co-existence' since it so often veered into out-right collaboration with imperalism. The Chinese People's Republic had itself only been created after lengthy guerrilla struggles under-taken without Soviet assistance and, after the Second World War, against Soviet advice. In a remarkable contradiction the same Chinese communists who had been largely independent of Stalin's directives when he was still alive, and who seized power against his wishes, began to parade as the defenders of his memory. If this line was taken in the hope of winning allies inside the Soviet and Eastern European Parties, its results were meagre. Neo-Stalinists in the Soviet Union and elsewhere had no more objection to collaboration with imperialist countries than had Stalin himself. The internal development of China departed in significant respects from the Stalinist model, even though it faced the same problems of primitive accumulation. China collectivized agriculture and made astonishing industrial progress without employing Stalin's terroristic campaigns against whole sections of the peasantry and working class. In the mid sixties, Mao Tse-tung instigated a period of mass criticism of bureaucracy and revisionism directed at the leading functionaries in the Party and state apparatus. This remarkable experiment, known as the Proletarian Cultural Revolution, mobilized millions of young people in political activity that was not controlled by the party even though it received some direction from above. The precise political issues involved were obscured by the fact that the rival groups all fervently proclaimed their support for Chairman Mao and the defeated opponents of Mao were convicted of patently false charges (Liu Shao-chi, the head of state, was described as having been a Japanese agent). Eventually the People's Liberation Army was used to restore order. However, the ambiguous results of the Cultural Revolution could not cancel out the novel way in which Mao had unleashed the mass of young people against the state and party bureaucracy in his bid to oust his political opponents, and the boldness of this political initiative had an impact far outside China.

Only one country in Eastern Europe came out in support of China in its conflict with the Soviet Union: Albania, the small and backward mountainous republic liberated by communist partisans during the Second World War. Rapprochement between the USSR and Yugoslavia, whose relations with Albania were traditionally hostile because of the old Yugoslav ambition to become the leading power in a Balkan Federation, helped to cement the alliance between China and Albania. Although Rumania remained neutral in the Sino-Soviet dispute, it enabled her government to resist Soviet pressure to attune its economy to Soviet needs.

The Yugoslav communists originally came to power against the will of the USSR with the victory of the guerrilla armies over Hitler's troops and over the Chetniks. They had adopted a different course from that taken by the USSR and its system when, after the beginning of the Cold War, they too were required to become mere subordinates and to use Stalinist methods. From the beginning of 1948 conflicts became more and more acute. In March 1948 the Soviet advisers who had helped with the socialist reconstruction of the economy and with the expansion and modernization of the army, were recalled. But the Yugoslav Communist Party did not allow itself to be forced to follow a specific direction. Its Fifth Party Congress in July 1948 confirmed the course which had been advocated by Moshe Pijade and Milovan Djilas as the theoretical leaders, and by Marshal Tito as the generally recognized political leader. The small pro-Stalinist opposition had no chance to manoeuvre, as it had no support among the peasants or in the working class. The USSR's breaking of economic relations with Yugoslavia in 1949 did make some serious changes in the planning system necessary, but it did not weaken the will of the party to build socialism independently. Of course, the rate of industrialization had to be reduced considerably. External economic relations were displaced to capitalist states.

The Yugoslav communists had taken into public ownership industrial production, mining, banking and insurance, transport and commerce, though some enterprises employing less than ten persons, such as restaurants, remained in private ownership. Agriculture was not collectivized though cooperatives competed with the prevailing small peasant holdings. Two features differentiated the Yugoslav economy from others in Eastern Europe. Firstly, the market was increasingly used to replace administrative-bureaucratic methods of regulating the economy, though overall planning was not abandoned. And from 1953 a system of workers' self-management was introduced into Yugoslav factories; a management was elected, with the Party nominating candidates and a fixed percentage of the trading surplus of the enterprise going to various public bodies from the central government to the local commune. In recoil from Stalinism the Yugoslav communists thus sought to give a more socialist content to their economic system. In the application of these experiments certain problems arose from over-emphasis on the market and a tendency for bureaucratic modes to remain in the political apparatus. Inequalities between regimes and groups of the working population did not disappear. But at least in the more developed states of the Federation (Slovenia, Croatia and Serbia) where there was an educated industrial work-force, the system did prove itself.

Since the Sixth Party Congress in 1952 the Yugoslav party has called itself the League of Communists which is designed to emphasize that it sees itself as intellectually and politically the leading force in society rather than as the unrestricted master of society. In 1953, the Socialist Federation of Working People joined it as a mass organization. The party programme decided upon at the Seventh Party Congress in April 1958, and reaffirmed at subsequent congresses, aimed to show the path along which the transformation of an already developed industrial society could develop into a communist classless society. However, the living standard of the Yugoslav worker was still considerably lower than that of the workers in the industrially advanced countries. But as industrialization proceeded – and it did so at a high rate up to the mid sixties – so did the living standards of the masses. As a consequence Yugoslav workers enjoyed better material standards than workers in the neighbouring capitalist states of Greece and Turkey. Comprehensive social welfare programmes still further improved the position of the Yugoslav worker and, as throughout the 'people's democracies' of Eastern Europe, there was a marked social promotion of workers in the state apparatus and an educational discrimination in favour of workers' children. Given its comparatively good record, Yugoslavia did not feel the need to insulate itself from the outside world. The one notable case of political repression in the early years was the imprisonment in 1955 of Milovan Djilas, a former leader of the Party, because he had written that the leading stratum of the party and state had actually become a new class. Otherwise room for discussion remained wider than elsewhere in Eastern Europe.

After Stalin's death, relations with the Soviet Union were normalized. The rapprochement with the USSR, the climax of which was the visit by Khrushchev in May 1955, was interrupted after the Hungarian uprising but was subsequently revived. The Yugoslav Trade Unions remained outside the two international organizations which formed at the time of the Cold War (a division of the workers' movement, which had subsequently been shown to have been encouraged by the CIA, and no doubt also the KGB). In 1949 the eastern World Federation of Trade Unions (WFTU) expelled the Yugoslav Trade Unions as agents of 'Titoist fascism', and the Yugoslavs refused to join the International Confederation of Free Trade Unions (ICFTU). The foreign policy of the Yugoslav government has been based on neutrality between the two power blocs and friendship with the nationalist regimes in the Arab countries, Africa and Asia. Considerable material aid was given to the Algerian FLN at the time of its struggle for national liberation. Yugoslavia has generally supported moves for a détente in Europe and for banning nuclear weapons.

In the mid sixties certain contradictory features of Yugoslavia's internal development have been more evident. The industrial rate of growth has slowed down somewhat and market forces have tended to accentuate inequality between different regions and social groups. Over half a million workers have gone abroad to work in Western Europe while an unemployment problem has appeared in the economy. In 1968 the powers of the secret police were curbed with the dismissal of the former Interior Minister, Ranković, and a wave of student unrest at deteriorating social conditions swept the universities. Although President Tito welcomed this spirit of the student movement, its most militant leaders have subsequently been disciplined and at least one of them, Mijanović, imprisoned. With growing economic difficulties, strikes have become quite common – although they are not yet formally legal – the government has tolerated this manifestation of a more independent working class. Another outlet for discontent has been a growth of nationalism in the member states which threatens to disrupt the prevailing balance of forces inside the institutions of the Federal Republic. Although Yugoslavia has often been regarded as a right-wing development within socialism, and though it has undeniably lost some of the original impetus that allowed it to break with Stalin, there still seems to be more space within its political structures for a more radical communist workers' current to develop than in the more tightly bureaucratized systems elsewhere in Eastern Europe.

The German working class faced the most difficult situation of all after the Second World War. Only a few of its leading members had survived the prisons and concentration camps of the Third Reich. The majority of its middle cadres were completely exhausted by years of imprisonment. The exiles could only return gradually and for a time their political activity was restricted according to the particular political wishes of the respective occupation power. At first they commanded great authority among the workers, as well as among other sections of the population. It was still generally known in all four occupation zones that they were members of the only political groups which had warned against the Third Reich from the beginning and had foreseen its movement towards war. People still remembered clearly that these were the only groups to have tried to oppose the Third Reich in a bitter illegal struggle; the bourgeois opposition had only appeared on the scene when it considered that there was a direct danger to the German Reich and to its ruling classes. Large sections of the population recognized the terrible misery at the end of the war to be a consequence of the politics of the Third Reich. The occupation powers opposed the attempts of the old illegal cadres to regroup immediately to form a unified working-class movement, and within the movement the exiles opposed these attempts also. The Soviet Union granted a 'licence' to the two bourgeois parties in its zone and to the SPD and the KPD. The Soviet

Union wanted at least to exercise discipline over the Communists before they permitted a unified party. After the Potsdam Agreement the other occupation powers followed the Soviet example in allowing parties. When the Communists were later pressing for unification with the SPD the mood had already changed: the isolated unification in April 1946 of the SPD and the KPD to form the Socialist Unity Party (SED) was understood by the workers in the other zones and in Berlin as the integration of the SPD into a Soviet-controlled KPD, although the KPD was at that time advocating a particular German road to socialism. The practical effect of this policy was to strengthen Kurt Schumacher's authority among the Social Democrat workers, Schumacher having been one of those to have proposed, along with the exiles returned from England, a hard line against the Communists. The Soviet Union's extraction of indemnifications from its occupation zone and the mass expulsion of Germans from the areas which had fallen to the states bound to the Soviet Union, that is, Poland and Czechoslovakia, caused a new flare-up of anti-Bolshevik resentment which the Third Reich had produced and the Eastern war had furthered. Because the Red Army had entered Germany with the clear memory of the inhuman crimes committed by the Third Reich against the Soviet and Polish population, its soldiers behaved in a less disciplined manner, in many areas, than the American and British troops. This, too, increased the unpopularity of the Soviet Union and therefore also of the Communists.

The German Communists cooperated energetically in the reorganization of economic and political life during the first period following the collapse in all four zones, and they made notable achievements. They also participated in the first *Länder* governments in the Western zone, generally in the most unrewarding ministries, virtually distributing hunger as equally as possible. When the Communists were pushed out of their positions with the extension of the Cold War from 1947–8, it was shown that they no longer had the basis in the working class of Western Germany which they still had at the provincial and local elections in 1946–7. As a result they were put out of action without opposition. It was characteristic of the further development that the authority of the individual communist officials, which resulted from their work in the factory councils and in the trade unions, could not be transferred to the West German Communist Party, whose influence declined steadily. In the first elections to the Federal Diet on 14 August 1949 it received only 5·7 per cent of the votes, as against 29·2 per cent for the SPD; but by 1953 the proportion had fallen to 2·2 per cent. The ban on the KPD in 1956 was directed against a party which hardly had any influence and which as an illegal group was bound to become a mere sect.

In the Soviet zone similar factors influenced the relationship between the Communist Party and the people, but the party developed in quite a different direction. In the West the occupation powers prevented any attempt at changing the social structure. Instead of consistently taking power from the hands of those social classes which had actively supported the Third Reich, they carried through a formal process of de-Nazification, treating lower and higher civil servants, manual workers, farmers, University professors, high-ranking judges and managers all as collaborators, and imposing fines on all of them. In contrast to this, the big landowners in the Soviet zone were expropriated under the law on land reform. Industry, the banks, and large-scale commerce were socialized; enterprises owned by Nazis or by capitalist companies controlled by Nazis were confiscated. The referendum on the expropriation of former Nazis in June 1945 in Saxony gave nearly 2·7 million in favour and only 700,000 against; at that time the result would hardly have been different in the Western zones. Because the SED seemed to guarantee the change of the German social structure it obtained between 44 and 50 per cent of the votes, according to the individual *Land*, in the provincial elections of October 1946.

The failure of the politics of reunification, however, the Soviet Union's policy on indemnification, arbitrary Stalinist rule, and above all the general scarcity, soon changed this situation. The Soviet Union continued to take valuable means of production out of its occupation zone. It even diverted reparations out of ongoing production, increasing this when it replaced 'dismantling' with the system of Soviet stock companies. Anti-Soviet feeling became more general; it was also directed against the SED and against members of that party influenced by Soviet policies. The Stalinist police in the occupation force, used as they were to the methods of the purges, were first of all, and most sharply, deployed against critical Communists and Social Democrats. The SED leaders provided a cover for these activities because they knew that they depended completely on the benevolence of the occupation power. The party leaders and the state apparatus thus became ever more isolated and tended increasingly to adopt the dogmatism and the methods of the occupiers. The Stalinization of the SED, its transformation into a 'party of a new type', was indicated in advance by this mechanism. This development also meant the end of intellectual freedom.

This was the situation in 1949 when, on the directive of the occupation powers, the two German half-states came into being. The partition of Germany was carried out by the Western powers on the basis of the London Conference of the Six Powers, and led to the formation of the Federal Republic. The USSR then transformed its zone, the poorer and more backward Eastern part of the country, into the German Democratic Republic (GDR). The constitution of the GDR, which was originally conceived as a project for an all-German constitution, stood in direct contradiction to existing reality from the first day of the state's existence onwards.

In the Federal Republic, Marshall Plan Aid initiated an increase in economic activity and in productivity which, with the added help of the armaments' boom in the other Western countries, and with the steady pressure of trade union struggles, raised the living standard of the West German workers to an exceptionally high level. There is, in fact, no parallel for this in the history of the German working class. In the GDR, however, despite considerable economic successes, the workers' living standards for long remained lower than the pre-war level. The extension of the social services, their guarantees by legislation, and above all the decisive improvement of education opportunities for working-class children did not alter the fact that income levels remained low, and that it was still not possible to use trade union channels or to participate democratically in political or economic decision-making. Any real analysis of the social and political situation was prevented and replaced by dogmatic formulae.

Directly after Stalin's death over-hasty collectivization policies, attacks on the church, and a further raising of work-norms led first to the strike of construction workers in Berlin and then to the events of 17 June 1953. The workers rose against the party which claimed to represent their interests, and the Red Army had to intervene to save the regime. In the face of the attractive high living standards in the capitalist West, the SED was not able to win a sufficiently strong basis in the working class and among the young intellectuals coming from the working class. The economic superiority of the Federal Republic was bound to increase if a steady stream of refugees robbed the GDR of its trainees as craftsmen, technicians and scientists. The material loss weighed double because the refugees' training and higher studies had generally been paid for out of GDR public funds. This, in turn, strengthened the party leaders' tendency to maintain Stalinist methods. Finally, it appeared to them to necessitate the complete cutting off of the GDR with the Berlin Wall. A considerable increase in economic activity has, however, taken place in the GDR within the framework of the planned economy, and in spite of planning methods which were previously completely bureaucratic and have only recently been improved. Living standards have risen and, as far as can be seen, will continue to rise.

The Stalinist development in the GDR since 1947 had a strong influence on developments in the Federal Republic. The KPD was practically crushed and the SPD was impelled towards the right. At the time of the formation of the Federal Republic, the workers were still struggling for a change of the capitalist social structure, as, for instance, in the big strike of November 1948. The founding conference of the German Confederation of Trade Unions in 1949 demanded economic planning, the nationalization of the leading industries, and complete self-management for the workers. As late as 1951, the co-determination law for the mining and the iron and steel industries was won with the threat of strikes. But when in 1952 the fight for legislation on factory constitutions was lost, the trade unions' urgency in advocating a transformation of the social structure ran out. They did still make successful efforts to win wage increases, shorter hours, and social improvements of all kinds, but in practice they were adjusting to the stabilization of the old social order and accepted the role which the Christian social doctrine and later the economic theoreticians of the SPD prescribed: not to be the class enemies of capital, but its 'social partners'. The spontaneous actions of the workers against incipient remilitarization in 1950–51 were neutralized by the hesitant attitude of the SPD and of the majority of trade union leaders. When the SPD agreed in 1956 to the changes in the constitution necessary for rearmament the workers' will to resist was already so weakened that there was no great opposition. The movement against arming the Bundeswehr with nuclear weapons which started soon after was isolated so effectively by the Social Democrats that in 1964 the Karlsbad party conference of the SPD agreed to the plans for a multilateral nuclear striking force, with only a few votes cast against.

The ruling ideology in the press and in education in the Federal Republic used denunciation of Stalinist methods in the GDR to reject all forms of social planning and reform. Similarly it used the performance of the GDR's nationalized industries, determined by its particular situation, as an argument against all forms of socialization, and the police system and the lack of freedom in the GDR as an argument against the very idea of a socialist society. After 1953 the SPD did nothing to counter such propaganda but began rather to accommodate itself to it following its defeat in the parliamentary elections of that year. By yielding to the moods of an affluent bourgeois society, the SPD prevented the workers from recognizing their objective situation as a social class dependent on the owners of the means of production. At a time when almost eighty per cent of the active population were wage-earners, the SPD no longer wanted to be a workers' party but a people's party. Of course, this desire did not change the fact that it remained objectively the party for which the workers and to an extent other groups of wage-earners voted; it only ceased to promote the development of the class-consciousness of the workers. In fact, it became an instrument for consolidating the influence of the ruling classes on the workers.

During the early sixties, there were hardly any effective socialist groupings in the Federal Republic. The left-wing socialists expelled from the SPD were disorganized and only influenced the universities through the Socialist Students' Union (SDS). The traditional consciousness of the German working-class movement was still to a certain extent kept alive in the trade unions, because there class problems remained confrontations over wages and hours. In late capitalist society, however, most social and political questions are determined by the intervention of the state. A merely trade-union consciousness which finds no political expression is therefore not even enough to guide the day-to-day struggles as soon as a political or economic crisis disturbs the calm of affluent capitalism.

Unfortunately the SPD was not alone among the European social democratic parties in this deviation from the socialist tradition, even though it expressed it more openly. The other working-class parties in the West experienced a severe setback as a result of the outbreak of the Cold War, the wave of re-Stalinization in the USSR, and the stabilization of capitalism in the West. In France, the PCF was strengthened by the resistance struggle and had become an equal partner of the SFIO when the first elections were held in October 1945. The PCF received 26·1 per cent of the votes, the SFIO 23·4 per cent. After the Communists participated in the government coalition with bourgeois parties their influence declined considerably. But the PCF remained the party in control of the reconstituted CGT. The CGT has remained the strongest industrial trade union to the present day. It is still a member of the World Federation of Trade Unions, whose nucleus is formed by the communist-led trade unions. The SFIO compromised itself in the Fourth Republic by accepting the ideology of the Cold War and supporting first the war in Indo-China and then the Algerian War. Small groups of intellectuals and a few trade union officials therefore split from it and formed the Socialist Unity Party (PSU). The trade union influence of the right-wing socialist-led Force Ouvrière is relatively small. The Christian trade union organization (CNT) was much stronger. It was in fact so radicalized by its participation in wage struggles that it decided in 1964 to abandon the designation 'Christian'. Indeed frequently its demands for social reforms and its representation of working-class interests are more radical than those of the CGT. Following the establishment of the Fifth Republic under de Gaulle the SFIO sought to make a left turn. For the Paris municipal elections of 1965 the PCF, PSU, and SFIO formed an electoral alliance in order to defeat the Gaullists. However, the ideology of the SFIO from Gaston Deferre to Guy Mollet corresponds to that of the SPD. The PCF remained a very different organization, though the fact that it was capable of voting credits for the colonial war in Algeria showed how far it was from being a revolutionary party.

In spite of its divisions, the French working-class movement won a level of wages in the period of the cyclical boom which was equivalent to that of the workers in the Federal Republic. Beyond that, the social service benefits, and above all the family allowances and old-age pensions, are much bigger. However, as later events were to show, these relatively important successes did not destroy the class consciousness of the French workers.

In Italy, too, the workers, especially those in the industrialized North, were able to improve their situation during the boom-period even if they did not attain the wage levels which exist, for instance, in France and Germany. The Communists, led by Palmiro Togliatti and Luigi Longo, were forced out of the government as a result of the Cold War, even though they had been prepared to help restore Italian capitalism and had not sought to exploit the relative strength and prestige built up during the war to press for socialist solutions. The socialists under Pietro Nenni stood fast against the Christian Democrats and their liberal and monarchist allies, in solidarity with their old allies in the illegal fight against Mussolini. The Social Democratic Party (PSDI), on the other hand, with Giuseppe Saragat as leader, split off from the PSI after 1947, maintaining that the alliance with the USA against the USSR should be defended. In the parliamentary elections of 1948 the Communists and Socialists were on a common platform as the 'Frente Democratico Populare' and received 30·7 per cent of the votes, while the future Social Democrats received 7·1 per cent. The Socialist-Communist alliance has been maintained up to the present day in the trade union movement; the Italian Confederation of Labour (CGIL) led by Socialists and Communists is still Italy's strongest trade union. Its nearest rivals are the Christian trade unions which are generally radical; the Italian trade union which belongs to the ICFTU is relatively weak.

The political alliance between the two working-class Italian parties was broken in 1956 after the Hungarian rising. Like the Social Democratic Party, the PSI also took part in the coalition government of the 'centre-left' led by the Christian Democrats. Because of this participation a small party split off from the PSI, the Socialist Party of Proletarian Unity (PSIUP), under Vecchietti and Lelio Basso. It found its support chiefly in the socialist youth organization, among trade union leaders and intellectuals. At the local elections in November 1964 the Communists received 25 per cent of the votes (as against 25·6 per cent in the parliamentary elections in 1963), the PSIUP received 2·9 per cent (in 1963 it was still part of the PSI), the PSI received 11·3 per cent (in 1963 14·2 per cent), and the Social Democrats 6·6 per cent (in 1963, 6·3 per cent). The Communists worked towards a popular front of the four working-class parties and the left wing of the Christian Democrats, and helped the Social Democrat Saragat to victory in the presidential elections at the end of 1964.

In two further European capitalist countries the Communists have a strong party and considerable influence in the trade unions. In Finland the party dominated by them received 25 per cent of the votes at the local elections in October 1964, the Social Democrats 27 per cent, and a small left-wing splinter-group one per cent. In Greece the Communist Party was banned, but, in contrast to the situation in the German Federal Republic, it was allowed to participate in elections as the United Democratic Left (EDA). There is no functioning Social Democratic Party in Greece. In all other West European countries social democracy is much stronger than communism or left-socialism. In most countries it has given up the notion of representing the class interests of workers and of other wage-earners and abandoned the idea that it must replace capitalist private property of the means of production by social ownership. However, in a large number of countries, the former left-wing of social democracy has split off to form parties which still promote socialist ideas – in addition to France and Italy such parties exist in Belgium, Norway, and Denmark, with somewhat similar pacifist-socialist parties in West Germany and the Netherlands. Generally these parties attract a small but not negligible vote.

In the Netherlands the right-wing social democratic Party of Labour received 1·75 million votes and 43 seats at the parliamentary elections of July 1963, as against 1·82 million votes and 48 seats in

1959; the Communists received 170,000 votes and 4 seats (in 1959, 140,000 and 3 seats), and the left-wing Pacifist-Socialist Party received 190,000 votes and 4 seats (in 1959, 110,000 and 2 seats). In Switzerland the parliamentary elections of October 1963 gave the Social Democrats 26·7 per cent of the votes (in 1959, 26·6 per cent), and the communist Party of Labour 2·2 per cent (in 1959, 2·8 per cent).

The Scandinavian social democratic parties who have been governing in their countries for decades and have made high living standards and extensive social services possible without changing the property relations, still hold on, in theory, to the objective of a socialist transformation of the whole society, at least in the left-wing of their organizations. In all three countries there are also small Communist parties, of which the Swedish party has gained most in importance in the last few years. It has overcome the dogmatism of the earlier years and is seeking a closer alliance with the left socialists of the other Scandinavian countries.

In Denmark and Norway the left-socialist parties are called Socialist People's Parties, and direct their efforts principally against their countries' membership of NATO. In Norway, at the 1963 parliamentary elections, the social democratic Workers' Party received 805,000 votes and 74 seats, the Socialist People's Party 39,000 votes and 2 seats, while the Communists obtained no seats but 49,000 votes. The Swedish parliamentary elections in September 1964 gave the Social Democrats 1·95 million votes and 117 seats (against 114 seats in 1960), the Communists 220,000 votes and 8 seats (as against 5 seats in 1960). In Denmark there were 1·1 million votes for the Social Democrats (76 seats), 150,000 votes for the Socialist People's Party (10 seats), and 30,000 votes for the Communists (no seats).

Whereas the leadership of the Socialist Party in Belgium is right-wing, the trade unions are militant; even the Christian unions have often shown great militancy in wage struggles. The mass strike in December 1960 and January 1963 against the 'Consolidation Bill' proposed by Eysken's government confirmed that the high standard of living enjoyed by Belgian workers has not in any way lessened their willingness to fight. In the parliamentary elections of March

1961 the Socialists obtained 16·7 per cent of the vote (in 1958 16·8 per cent) and the Communists 3·1 per cent (in 1958 1·9 per cent). At the turn of the year 1964–5 a new left-socialist party was formed out of the radical wing around the Walloon-federalist group and around the newspapers *La Gauche* and *Links*. A small pro-Chinese party has split off from the Communists.

The fragmentation of the working-class movement in Europe is particularly disadvantageous in the context of the links between the six European states (European Economic Community, Euratom, and the Coal and Steel Community), because important economic decisions are made in these institutions which also have consequences for social policy. If there is no cooperation between the organizations of the working-class movement, no counterweight to the representatives of the employers' and governments' interests can be created. The strongest working-class parties of France and Italy, the PCF and PCI, were initially excluded from the European Parliament, and the strongest trade unions in both these countries, the CGT and CGIL, were not drawn into its consultations. While the connections between the large firms are increasing steadily, the workers' interests, even in questions of social policy, cannot be represented within the institutions of the EEC in such circumstances. In France and Italy Communist, Socialist, Social Democrat, and Christian trade unions are fighting industrial struggles together. It is difficult to understand why the unions which belong to the ICFTU and the Christian organizations should not be allowed to cooperate with the unions in the WFTU. But with all bureaucratic mass organizations it takes some time before they free themselves from the old routines and adapt themselves to a new situation. However, in general, trade unions tend to be more responsive to the immediate interests of the masses than political parties.

Another urgent problem which faces the working class is that created by the large-scale internal migration of labour from the less developed Southern regions to the more developed Northern ones; parallel to this is the immigration from former colonial territories in Britain, France and the Netherlands. In most European countries about a fifth of the working class is composed of such immigrants and they are usually the most exploited section of the proletariat and sub-proletariat. They are invariably denied elementary political and trade union rights, either legally or in practice. They are used by the ruling class as a factor of division within the working class – though this problem is somewhat less acute in France because of the generally more advanced political consciousness of the French workers. Clearly all workers' organizations should fight for the rights of these specially exploited sections of the class, and combat chauvinism within their own ranks. It has always been the goal of the workers' movement to fight the divisions and discriminations which bourgeois society itself creates within it – whether on grounds of sex, race, religion or nationality – and by doing so to develop its own ability to lead society and overthrow capitalism.

While the Second World War tended to bring together the different political wings of the workers' movement, the Cold War forced them apart. The periodic barbaric relapses of the Soviet bureaucratic dictatorship have always helped to widen the two main camps of the workers' movement. In the past the Social Democratic parties have always displayed an ultimate loyalty to their own bourgeois state while the Communist parties have shown an equivalent loyalty to the Soviet state. However, already in the last years of Stalin's domination of the Communist movement, some parties had openly declared the possibility of a parliamentary transition to socialism – notably the British Communist Party in its programme *The British Road to Socialism*. On 14 November 1957 the Moscow Conference of Communist Parties declared that in its opinion a socialist transformation of society might be brought about in the parliamentary-democratic capitalist states by the winning of an electoral majority. With this declaration (repeated several times since) one of the weightiest reasons for the division and hostility between Social Democratic and Communist parties has been removed. While more cooperation between the two types of parties can be envisaged, the more classical revolutionary concept deriving from Marx's interpretation of the Commune has passed to the different currents of the new left.

Up to the First World War, the workers' movement was absorbed in winning elementary democratic rights and imposing on reluctant bourgeois states the bare minimum social conditions necessary to mitigate the remorseless process of capital accumulation. Although most working-class movements in Europe by this time proclaimed adherence to the ideas of socialism, their defective understanding and application of these ideas became only too apparent with their capitulation to chauvinism at the outbreak of the war. Even after the wholesale slaughter and misery which imperialism imposed on the people of Europe during the war, the workers' movement was only politically developed enough to seize power at the 'weak link' of the imperialist chain – the sprawling, backward Tsarist Empire, with its vast peasant masses who had as yet been scarcely touched by the actions of the Marxist revolutionaries. Instead of the socialist revolution being able to inherit highly developed forces of production from capitalism, it assumed power in a country where the bourgeoisie had not yet accomplished the tasks of primitive capital accumulation. Moreover, it confronted the active intervention of every imperialist power – though the solidarity of the workers' movement did force an end to these interventions. The isolation of the Bolsheviks in backward Russia badly crippled the revolution. Stalin, who usurped the power of the soviets, channelled the formidable energies released by the revolution into a forced collectivization and industrialization which fused the achievements of modern science with barbarities which paralleled those of Russia's past.

In the rest of Europe, despite armed workers' risings in Berlin and Budapest, Helsinki and Munich immediately after the First World War, capitalism was able to suppress and contain the challenge of the workers' movement. The major Social Democratic sections of the movement continued to press for reforms and ameliorative economic measures. They proved quite unable to counteract the social and economic misery of the masses during the great capitalist depression. The distortions of Stalinism disoriented and divided the revolutionary sections of the working class and furnished the social democratic leaders with an effective alibi for their betrayals. Fascism was able to win important victories for these reasons – above all in Germany and Spain, two countries where circumstances appeared to favour the workers' movement. During the Second World War the enormous sacrifices of the Soviet people made the victory over fascism possible and throughout Europe the workers' movement recovered its vitality in the struggle against the occupying power. The partisans led victorious social revolutions in Yugoslavia and Albania, while the Soviet Red Army swept over the rest of Eastern Europe liberating it from the Nazis. Stalin's eagerness to do a deal with the bourgeois democracies led to the bloody suppression of the Greek revolution and the restoration of a badly shaken capitalist order in Italy, France, Austria, Finland and West Germany. In the aftermath of the war the Stalinist caricature of socialism was imposed on Eastern Europe – though Yugoslavia successfully resisted Soviet domination – while US-sponsored neo-capitalism sought to integrate the workers' movement in Western Europe. However, there have already been many signs in both East and West that the historic mission of the workers to liberate themselves and all other oppressed groups has not been successfully suppressed either by the bureaucracy of the East or the consumer ideology of the West.

Rapid industrial progress in the Soviet Union offered an example to the peoples of the former colonial and semi-colonial territories. Industrialization by means of planning and social ownership developed more quickly than under capitalist private enterprise. Thus the example of the first workers' revolution influenced a development which led to the revolutions in China, Cuba and South East Asia. In further developing the revolution that began in Petrograd in 1917 the socialist revolutionaries of the Third World have improved upon the model that was offered to them. But although they have shown many of the deformations of Stalinism to be avoidable, they are still prevented from installing an integral socialism by the low level of development of the productive forces, and the size and situation of the working class in these countries has not allowed it to assume unfettered leadership of the revolutionary state. But, in its turn, the example in South East Asia of heroic and successful revolutionary struggle against the apparently invincible might of the United States has encouraged the rebirth of a revolutionary tradition within the European workers' movement.

Postscript, 1971
The European
Working-Class Movement
between 1965 and 1971

The first German edition of this book was completed early in 1965. It has therefore become necessary to ask if the end of the sixth and the beginning of the seventh decade of our century have led to developments requiring a basic revision of the book's approach.

There is no doubt that the half decade which has passed since the first German edition – it has meanwhile appeared in numerous European languages and in Japan – does make a number of additions necessary.

The European economic recession of 1965–7, and the political crises of 1968, accentuated tendencies which had already become apparent in both the capitalist states and the socialist countries during the earlier period of deceptive stability, in the second half of the fifties and the beginning of the sixties. But they also suggested the limits of these tendencies. The current forms of consciousness and behaviour of working-class parties and trade union organizations seem to be relatively rigid. As long as no major economic or political catastrophe occurs – such as, in the past, the First World War, the depression of 1929/30, the rise of the Third Reich and the outbreak of the Second World War – the currently fixed balance between capitalism in the West and socialism in the East will encourage the illusion among the reformist labour parties of Western Europe that this state of affairs is a permanent one. Added to this illusion is the quite mistaken conviction that capitalism has achieved a stability without contradictions and thus cannot be superseded. Meanwhile socialism is still dominated by bureaucratic forms as well as lagging behind technologically. The defeats which national liberation movements have inflicted on American and European imperialism since the Second World War – and which they continue to inflict in the present (e.g. in South Vietnam) – have so far made only a limited impact on the mentality and politics of the major working-class parties. Despite the rise of the movement of solidarity with the anti-imperialist struggle in South East Asia there is still a widespread belief in the stability of the capitalist order in the West.

Throughout capitalist Europe the last few years have seen a significant growth in the economic militancy of the working class. In countries such as Sweden and West Germany, the passivity of the working class has been broken and the strike weapon has been re-discovered by the trade unions. Within the workers' organizations a certain spirit of revolt has appeared among the rank and file that had previously been eclipsed by the combined influence of the Cold War and the 'miracles' of late capitalism. In countries where there was already a more vigorous economic struggle, such as France, Italy and Britain, there has been a marked increase in the incidence of strikes combined with the re-discovery of more effective and militant forms of proletarian action against capital – notably the mass occupation of factories by workers. The following figures for strikes in Italy and Britain serve as a rough barometer of the economic class struggle:

Days lost per thousand persons in mining, manufacturing, construction and transport industries (*Source:* ILO)

	1963–7 (average)	1969
Italy	1,050	4,110
Britain	180	510

Although this strike wave brought in its train a certain radicalization at the base of the trade unions it did not produce a crisis in the bourgeois political regime or lead to any permanent changes in the political organization of the working class. The course of the French class struggle was much sharper. The momentous clash between ten million workers occupying their factories and the bourgeois state in May 1968 was a dramatic reminder that the revolutionary struggle of the European working class against the capitalist social order was by no means extinguished, whatever the snares and obstacles that have strewn its path. However, the immediate effects of this upsurge on the established workers' organizations were not far-reaching. As we shall see, the positions of the workers' parties at the level of elections and governments does not yet reflect the new spirit at the base.

In Great Britain, the legacy of the Conservative Government in domestic affairs and foreign policy confronted Wilson's Government elected in October 1964 with some immediate and harsh choices. As a typical Labour Government it did not seek to challenge the basic relations of production. British imperialism no longer possessed the resources to make significant economic reforms a possibility. The Wilson Government therefore eschewed any attempt to tamper with the social structure. In foreign policy dependence on the United States led the Labour Government to ally itself with the global protector of capitalism in its war against all signs of social revolution in the Third World.

The failures of the Wilson Government and the consequent disillusionment of the working class took place in a political context where there was no convincing alternative to the Labour Party as the political expression of working-class interests. The new left had not yet learnt to combine theoretical reflection with the incipient radicalization of the rank and file in the trade union movement. They did not get beyond more or less abstract ideas combined with demonstrations opposing imperialist politics: a pattern characteristic of students and intellectuals who are, as yet, unable to formulate a programme that can be understood by industrial workers and translated into political organization. As we shall see, it is the absence or weakness of any alternative which largely explains the workers' loyalty to their established organizations, however inadequate the latter may be.

The policy of the Labour government after 1964 never went beyond the framework of the mere administration of overall capitalist interests. In practice, it merely attempted to use the credit it possessed in the working-class movement and the trade unions to tame them and integrate them into the existing system. Nonetheless the

Labour Government always remained (even in the eyes of many radical groups) a 'lesser evil' than Conservative rule. The devaluation of the pound in 1967 was a belated rationalizing step to re-establish British competitiveness on the world market. From the point of view of capitalist interests it was an objective necessity. Right-wing parties, concerned about retaining their potential votes in the middle classes, are quite happy to leave such measures to governments created by reformist parties, especially if the latter themselves regard these measures as desirable. The reactionaries then, of course, exploit them demogogically in order to regain power. But because the devaluation of the pound was preceded and combined with a so-called prices and incomes policy (which in practice only affected wages), it became an attack on the trade unions and on the social gains of the English working class. The Prices and Incomes Board, set up on the initiative of George Brown, thus anticipated the political direction which the German Social Democratic Minister Schiller subsequently tried to implement in the Federal Republic of Germany. The 'early warning system' for wage demands, agreed to by the Government and the General Council of the TUC on 2 September 1965, was from its inception a move in the direction of the subsequent Prices and Incomes Act of 27 June 1968. The authority of the Labour leadership was still sufficient to obtain approval for this policy of wage restriction at the Trade Union Congress in 1965 (5·25 to 3·32 million votes) and in 1966 (5 to 3·9 million). The parliamentary majority of the Labour Party was initially so small that extreme party discipline seemed imperative. The need to keep Conservative opposition at bay meant that for many Labour activists all other considerations had to be held within bounds. The elections following the dissolution of Parliament in March 1966, however, substantially increased Labour's majority: they won back 47·9 per cent of the votes (as opposed to 44·1 per cent in 1964), the Conservatives dropped from 43·4 per cent in 1964 to 41·9 per cent, the Liberals from 11·9 per cent to 8·6 per cent. But despite this stronger position neither the Labour leadership nor the left broke with the pattern already established.

The transport workers under Frank Cousins opposed the subordination of the workers to the interests of capitalism from the start, but their strong opposition only gained majority support at the Trade Union Congress in September 1967, where this policy of deflation favouring the employers was denounced (4·9 millions against 3·5 who persisted in following the Goverment). The more militant unions now returned to demands for structural changes leading to a socialist economic policy.

But a few weeks later, at the Labour Party Conference, the Government again managed, despite opposition from many trade unions, to win a narrow majority for its policy.

The strong position of the leadership was also demonstrated when Wilson obtained party support for a renewed application to join the EEC, though the French Government, whose foreign policy he failed to take into account, proved less compliant. In foreign affairs the Labour Government persisted in its unhesitating reliance on the waning force of US imperialism to the bitter end. It is a great indictment of the moral standing of the Labour Party that it did not until 1967 disassociate itself in any way from the genocidal US war in Vietnam, and even then the passage of a Conference resolution had no effect on the Government.

In 1968 a Conference resolution was also passed rejecting the Government's Prices and Incomes Bill but to equally little effect; the Government went forward with its incomes policy and social service cuts while the Conference promised the Government continued support despite disagreements. Wilson therefore believed he could continue his course. In January 1969 the *Report of the Royal Commission on Trade Unions* ('The Donovan Report'), recommended various measures for taming the economic militancy of the trade unions. By this time the Engineering Workers as well as the Transport Workers consistently opposed all forms of wage restraint and were led by men more responsive to the militancy of the shop-stewards and local organizers than their predecessors. The Donovan Report sought to reduce the large number of unofficial strikes by tightening up the structure of the trade union movement and then making the unions responsible before the law for the actions of their members. The Wilson Government then published a White Paper, *In Place of Strife*, which endorsed many of the proposals of the Donovan Report and proposed to introduce legislation to implement them. The foundations were thus laid for the anti-union Industrial Relations Act. This was to be implemented however only by a Conservative Government under Edward Heath in 1971. The opposition of the large trade unions to Wilson's plans in the delicate period before a General Election forced the Government to back down. A further White Paper on Productivity, Prices and Incomes in December 1969 showed the fundamentally anti-working class orientation of the Government once again. It sought to tie wage increases to the growth of productivity while allowing prices to escalate unchecked.

The Labour Cabinets from 1964 to 1970 thus provided a model for the way in which a previously reformist labour party, whose leaders conceive of their organization as a 'national party' rather than a 'class party', can, when it becomes the government, sink to the level of merely serving the everyday interests of capitalism. It is then bound to lose power because it has, through concessions to the ruling classes, long been weakening the class which first believed itself to be represented by it. The Labour Party (contrary to the predictions of the opinion polls) inevitably paid the price in the election on 18 June 1970: the Conservatives received 13·1 million votes (46 per cent), the Liberals 2·1 million, and Labour only 12·1 million (43 per cent). Why should the workers and white-collar workers bother overmuch about commitment to the Labour Party when it was only a slightly 'lesser evil' than the Conservatives on only a few questions, and when its handling even of these questions was not immediately comprehensible to them?

Nevertheless, despite the shock of Labour's defeat and despite its obsolescence as a reformist party, the structure of the Party and the unions remains unchanged. On certain questions, particularly those linked to the workers' economic struggle, it had been possible to ignore the Labour Party but not to replace it with any more adequate political expression of the working class. The Labour Party Conference in September 1970 passed a resolution declaring that the Parliamentary Party and leadership should henceforth be bound by Conference decisions – but, as so often before, this could not be enforced in practice. If the more important groups of the new left could only adjust their language and theory to the practical needs of the trade union opposition to the Labour Party they could help trade union militants get beyond attitudes only related to short term interests. If British workers can develop a political response to the policies of Heath's Conservative Government this could lead to a regeneration of the British labour movement.

In the smaller capitalist states of Western Europe there were similar problems, with slight national variations. Here too, no serious consequences arose out of the shock felt in capitalist states of the 1966–7 economic recession and the onslaught of the rebellion of young intellectuals and students in 1967–8, or out of the challenge to political forms of government in the socialist states due to the breakdown of old bureaucratic structures in Czechoslovakia in 1968 and the far-reaching effects of the Sino–Soviet dispute.

In Belgium, the loss of prestige which the Socialist Party suffered through its policy of coalition with the Social Christian Party, and the problems involved in a constitutional reform regulating the language conflict between the Walloons and the Flemish, reduced its share of the votes to 28·3 per cent in the 1965 elections. The Communists increased theirs to 4 per cent, and the Walloon Workers' Party (under strong Trotskyist influence) was able to attract 1 per cent of the vote. The brief interlude of the Liberal–Social Christian coalition failed to alter this picture. The 1967 elections produced almost the same results for the reformist Socialist Party (in which a left opposition is still quite considerable) and for the Communists. In December 1970 the re-established Social Democrat–Christian Socialist coalition at least managed to produce a constitutional solution to the problem of regionalization and cultural autonomy for the three nationalities (although the question of Brussels remained unsettled). The small Belgian Trotskyist Party founded in 1977 is unlikely to gain electoral significance, although it possesses a notable theorist in the person of Ernest Mandel.

In the Netherlands, too, the social democrat Party of Labour paid the price of its opportunist policy of coalition. It suffered a considerable setback in the 1967 elections, while the small Communist Party made minor gains and the Socialist Pacifist Party held its vote. The rebellion of the younger generation showed itself in the rapid rise of fluid parties with progressive tendencies (on foreign policy, education and armaments). The coalition of bourgeois parties which followed led to a revival of socialist thought in the Party of Labour. This process culminated in the creation of a right-wing Social Democrat Party in 1971, which has since become a partner in the coalition. But it could do nothing to halt the influence of the regenerated Party of Labour or the slow but continuous rise of the Communists.

In Luxemburg the Social Democrats' participation in a coalition government with the Christian Social Party led to a drop to 32 per cent of the votes in the December elections of 1968. The Communists, despite their total support for the Soviet invasion of Czechoslovakia, increased to 15·5 per cent of the votes. Here too, the coalition of bourgeois parties which has since held power could give a chance to the left opposition within the Social Democratic party.

In those Scandinavian countries which are members of NATO, the process of displacement and partial regeneration in the labour movement has taken a similar course. In Norway, neither the 1965 nor the 1969 elections broke the absolute majority of votes for the three workers' parties, but they were cheated of a parliamentary majority by the nature of the electoral system. In 1965, the number of votes for the Socialist People's Party (SFP) rose to 4 per cent at the expense of the governing Social Democratic party, while the Communists hovered around the 1 per cent limit. It was precisely this, however, which enabled a combination of all the bourgeois parties to win a narrow parliamentary majority and form a government for the first occasion in a long time. The situation remained much the same in 1969, except that almost 3 per cent of the SFP returned to the Social Democratic party. This was to avoid a repeat of the previous unwanted outcome, and also because the left wing of the labour party had increased its influence. It was, however, not enough to bring the distribution of seats into line with the distribution of votes. The bourgeois bloc was therefore not succeeded by a Social Democratic government until 1971. Even then, this was the result of internal conflicts within the bourgeois bloc.

In Denmark Larsen's Socialist People's Party (SVP) rose to almost 11 per cent of the votes in the 1966 elections and 'tolerated' a government of Social Democrats, who had lost 4 per cent of their votes. The policy of the Social Democratic cabinet, which was all too ready to make concessions to capital (and to NATO), caused a split in the unity of the SVP. The Socialist Left broke off under the leadership of Moltke and forced the SVP to give up its policy of toleration. In the 1968 elections, all four socialist parties suffered heavy losses. The Social Democrats sank to 34 per cent, the SVP to 6 per cent, the Socialist Left to 2 per cent and the Communists to 1 per cent of the potential votes, so that here, too, political power transferred to a coalition of bourgeois parties. Groups which would once, in the vocabulary of the Third International, have been called 'ultra-left' largely found expression within the Socialist Left, as was also the case with the Norwegian SVP. The general inflationary trend of the period of oligopolistic capitalism has meant a drop in real wages, and this has reinforced class-oriented thinking among the Social Democrats too. The 1971 elections boosted the Social Democrats up to 37 per cent and the SVP, which is strongly opposed to entry into the Common Market, to 9 per cent, while the left-wing socialists received 1·6 per cent and the Communists 1·4 per cent of the votes.

In Iceland the 1967 elections increased the vote of the Social Democrats (despite their coalition with the bourgeois parties) from 14 per cent to almost 16 per cent. A left-wing socialist-communist bloc went up from 15 per cent to 19·7 per cent. Growing opposition to the US military base has accentuated this trend even more in 1971. A new coalition government including Communists has been formed to bring about its closure.

In the three states – Switzerland, Austria and Sweden – which are formally neutral, but where government policy has always been aimed at forming blocs with the great capitalist powers (and thus, up to now, with their leading world power, the USA) the situation in these years has been similar.

In Switzerland the 1967 elections produced a slight setback for the Social Democrats (participants in the Government and the Federal Council). They only retained 51 of their 53 seats in a parliament of 200. The (Communist) Labour party (PdA) rose slightly from 4 to 5 seats, although its influence is still only significant in the French-speaking cantons. The German-speaking workers still allow their illusion of superiority to the numerous foreign (especially Italian and Spanish, but also Yugoslavian and Turkish) immigrant workers to chain them to the anti-bolshevik-conservative policy of their union leaders, who want to avoid any strike action whatsoever. They are now faced, however, with the growing opposition of young intellectuals and students in addition to the PdA. The Social Democrats were irresolute in their opposition to the new chauvinism. In one canton (Zug) they even supported a proto-fascist organized call for a plebiscite in 1970, without being expelled from the Party. As a result, in the 1971 elections they lost a further 5 seats, picked up by the fast-growing chauvinist parties. The Communist Workers' Party retained its 5 seats.

In Austria, the Social Democrats were compromised by a case of corruption involving the ex-Social Democratic trade union leader Oula. They came out of the 1966 elections weaker than before, even though the small Communist Party (in all except one electoral district) gave them their support. The Austrian People's Party, whose parliamentary strength was only slightly greater than that of the Social Democrats, henceforth governed alone. The Communists, meanwhile, lost a substantial number of cadres through disagreements over the Czech crisis after 1968. The People's Party's monopoly of power gave the Social Democrats a chance to win 7 seats in 1970 and thus outnumber them by 2 seats. The Social Democrats formed a government under Bruno Kreisky, a man who long ago renounced all the Marxist traditions of his younger years. They only have a majority, however, because a small 'liberal' party supports them in parliament. The Liberal Party is a 'middle-class' party which includes many ex-National Socialists. This results in similar moral taints and internal party differences to those experienced by the West German Social Democrats through participation in Kiesinger's cabinet. In terms of real politics – i.e. the distribution of power among the various classes – this change of government has therefore made little difference. The (admittedly weak) opposition within the Social Democratic Party, however, especially college students, secondary-school students and some sections of the youth organization, as well as a number of the older social democratic trade unionists, was able to clarify its programme through this situation. The 1971 elections gave the Socialists a slight majority in parliament and this could release them from Liberal pressure; the Communists obtained 1·5 per cent of the votes.

In Sweden the local and regional elections in 1966 dealt a serious blow to the Social Democrats and increased the Communist vote to 7 per cent. In the national elections in 1968, however, they suffered a defeat because of the Czech crisis, and retained only 3 per cent of this vote. The 1970 national elections reduced the Social Democrats from 50·1 per cent of the votes in 1968 to 45·3 per cent, while the Communists received 5 per cent. From this point onwards, the Communists 'tolerated' Olaf Palme's Social Democratic government. This step was all the easier to justify because of a shift to the left by the Social Democratic Party under pressure from the oppositional younger generation. As early as the Party conference in 1969 (where Palme succeeded Erlander as head of the party and the government), this led to the recognition of North Vietnam, the condemnation of the American war, and the preparation of a left-wing reformist programme for the government. In the Swedish Communist Party there are strong factional struggles between the old dogmatic Stalinist groups (in particular the workers in North Sweden) and a very flexible party leadership. Some of their students show a preference for Maoist tendencies; these also have a small party organization of their own. There has been no way of preventing the growth of the communists, however, especially in view of their skilful policy in the trade unions, which has benefited from the restiveness of the rank and file. Nonetheless their strength is unlikely to be sufficient to force the Social Democrats to adopt a policy which serves the interests of the workers and which, however reformist, would be sufficiently energetic to save them from electoral defeat.

The only European capitalist state which really occupies a neutral position between the two blocs is Finland. It can hardly afford to turn anti-Soviet because of the proximity of its erstwhile occupying power, the USSR. Furthermore the USSR abandoned the occupation with amazing rapidity, including the military base which it maintained for some time but then gave up. Finland's chronic agricultural crisis and the fall of wood prices on the world market, which had negative effects on the whole of the economy, have gradually reduced the influence of the working-class parties, which have long participated in government coalitions. In the elections from 1966 to 1970, the Social Democrats dropped from 27·2 per cent to 23·8 per cent of the votes, and the Communists (the Democratic Union) from 21·2 per cent to 18·1 per cent. There is no likelihood of a return to aggressive anti-Communism by the Social Democrats, although this is advocated by a small group in the party. In the Communist Party the elaboration of a clear strategy has been obstructed for years by the chronic factional struggles with old Stalinists.

A small European country, Malta, once a British possession, is currently trying to move to a neutral position and discard its role as an important NATO naval base. NATO has withdrawn its command headquarters following the narrow victory of the Labour Party in 1971. The Labour Party had already acquired 6 new seats in the 1965 elections, but was still weaker than the pro-British, conservative, 'Nationalist' party. It is totally unpredictable whether this Labour government will succeed in its coalition with the Arabic states in power politics. Its problem is to maintain the island's economic viability at a time when its docks are rapidly losing their former significance.

Since the first edition of this book the working-class movements in two European states have lost their legality through subjection to fascist military dictatorships (Greece and Turkey). Both are (and were) members of NATO (and still enjoy its support) even though NATO is allegedly meant to serve the preservation of democracy. The leaders of many formerly reformist social democratic parties in the larger NATO states are passive in the defence of workers' interests but are always ready to support anti-Communist hysteria. The events in these two countries show how their policy can permit the stabilization of fascist regimes in allied states.

In Greece, only a very limited restoration of civil and legal forms of government followed the defeat of EAM and ELAS by British imperialism shortly before the end of the Second World War and the victory, with US protection, of pro-royalist troops over the resistance movement in the second civil war. The social classes and political forces which supported the fascist Metaxas dictatorship and then collaborated in the Nazi occupation were once more safely in possession of power. Nevertheless the left-wing intellectuals and the Communists, who had been banned as an independent party, managed to create a formally legal counter-force in EDA. They thus made possible the revival of the former petit-bourgeois-peasant Venizelists, who formally took over the government for a brief period in 1963 as the Centre Union under Papandreou. This was achieved after a short interlude thanks to the support of EDA, which largely gave up independent appearances in order to help them. The popular leader of EDA, the poet Grigoris Lambrakis, was murdered by the police in the course of the election campaign and the murder was legalized by the courts. In 1965 the King managed, by clever manipulation, to exploit the unsuccessful efforts of left-wing followers of the Centre Union. He confronted the extremist clique of reactionary officers and generals with his own faction in the army, and won some of the Centre Union's leaders, as well as the most reactionary wing of the grand bourgeoisie, over to his side. Papandreou's cabinet was replaced by unstable and increasingly corrupt governments leading to EDE, the right-wing Restoration party. With the threat of new elections in 1967, which would doubtless have produced a vast majority for the core of the Centre Union and EDA, Kanelopoulos was named as the new head of government so that the Crown could manipulate the elections. But even manipulated elections seemed too uncertain an experiment to the officers' clique (probably rightly so from their point of view). Generals and colonels both prepared for a putsch based on NATO plans in case of a conflict with the USSR or a left-wing victory. On 21 April 1967, the colonels, acting more quickly and decisively, took power. EDA was banned, as were the Communists, who despite the murder of Lambrakis had rightly been prepared to form an alliance with Papandreou in the mere hope of an electoral victory for his Central Union. They thus suffered a total defeat without any resistance. They had overlooked the basic problem of any united front policy: in historically decisive situations a united front depends for its success on independent working-class participation. It must be remembered that the legal weapons of electoral participation can only lead to victory if the masses are willing to engage in an active extraparliamentary struggle. When it becomes necessary, the petit-bourgeois partners in the coalition must be forced to follow. The working-class parties which are prepared to fight must therefore never rely on, or subordinate themselves to, the utterances of bourgeois-democratic politicians. Petit-bourgeois democrats, however radical they may be in words, lack the serious will and ability personally to declare and organize the armed struggle of the masses against the bourgeoisie and the traditional sections of the state apparatus. Since this time, the fascist dictatorship of Papadopoulos has dominated the Greek scene. The brutal terror of mass arrests was largely successful in smashing the organization of the Communists. Although the core of an opposition is beginning to reappear, the illegal reorganization of the Communists and their allies is today still characterized by the struggle between divergent tendencies and factions. These are an inevitable consequence of any discussion on the causes after a catastrophe of this kind. The illegal struggle stands a greater real chance of success, however, than was the case in Germany before 1945, because of the migrant workers from Greece in West Germany and Switzerland. They form an industrial reserve army, which is not integrated into society, and can thus return home in periods of conjunctural imbalance. There can only really be any hope, of course, if there is at least a relative restoration of the unity of the working-class opposition, and if the workers in other European states can wage a successful struggle against their governments to put an end to the support which the fascists in Greece still receive from all the other NATO states. Obviously the Communist Party of Cyprus, which is still legal and relatively strong, has abandoned its efforts for integration into Greece following the fascist coup. In the 1967 presidential elections it supported Makarios.

In Turkey the labour movement has never managed to mobilize more than relatively small cores of intellectuals and qualified industrial workers. Its legality has always been relatively limited and threatened through a ban on Communist activity. The majority of workers are still too tied to the thought forms of their agrarian background to be reachable – except in isolated industrial centres. Despite this the Labour Party, which is led by Marxist intellectuals, attracted about 3 per cent of the votes in both the 1965 and the 1969 elections. In contrast, the revolutionary student movement, which gained greater influence in 1970, leans towards direct action inspired by Castro and Mao. The military regime, which came to power in 1971 through an army putsch, has destroyed the semi-legality of the Labour Party. By means of terrorism it aims to liquidate completely any attempts to form a socialist movement. The problem of migrant workers, however, offers the communist-oriented illegal organization similar opportunities to those of the Greek revolutionary movement. Unemployed Turkish peasant sons are deported *en masse* to West Germany and Switzerland. In these countries they can at least become acquainted with the organizational possibilities of a working-class movement, and because they are not 'integrated' there they have to return to Turkey.

In the old fascist states, whether directly involved in the NATO system (Portugal) or drawn in through military treaties with the USA (Spain), the tendencies which were clearly apparent before 1965 have developed further. Portugal managed to solve the problem of a successor to Salazar without significant modifications – even the changes in the form of its colonial administration are relatively unimportant. The influence of the illegal activity of socialist forces (with the Communist Party as the most stable grouping) has essentially been limited to students and intellectuals. In Spain, however, progress in industrialization has considerably improved the possibilities for the working-class movement and the socialists. It has also led to a new outbreak, among a number of the younger priests, of the social contradictions in Spanish Catholicism. The illegal organization of the traditional working-class movement must henceforth approach the problem of alliances in a new way. A section of the higher clergy and the managers of Spanish capital, which has been reinforced by capital imports from America (and recently also from West Germany), have gathered around Opus Dei, which supports a relative modernization of the forms of political rule (in contrast to the old fascist forces), but naturally wants to preserve the basic elements of fascism. Meanwhile, groups are constantly forming among the younger priests (of various orders), which consciously represent workers' interests. They support a joint struggle for democratic interests against capitalist society with the illegal Communist and

Socialist forces, both among students and in the factories. The workers are constantly becoming reinvolved in social struggles and strikes, partly employing semi-legal forms within the pseudo-trade-union organization and partly using their own factory committees. The influence of the revolutionary movement is constantly increasing among workers and students, although unsuccessful actions are inevitably followed by setbacks. It is true that, because of their strict illegality, the parties of the working class are still relatively weak in terms of membership, especially the Communist Party which, although it has the best underground organization, is split at its highest level by a dispute over the Soviet occupation of Czechoslovakia. All of them, however, have close connections with these movements. If Franco's regime totters because of an internal crisis, the Spanish working-class movement will therefore begin under better auspices than could have been supposed even a few years ago. Here too the migrant worker problem will be of assistance, for the number of Spanish workers in highly industrialized European states is very large.

In the classic country of the capitalist 'economic miracle', the Federal Republic of Germany, the elections on 19 September 1965 seemed to give a complete and lasting confirmation of the political atmosphere of the Restoration. The SPD had almost completely fallen into line with this by its adoption not only of the Godesberg Programme but also of the Federal Government's claim to the 'sole right' to represent both German states in 1960. The CDU/CSU, the bourgeois party which had governed the Federal Republic since its foundation, received 47·6 per cent of the votes (compared to 45·3 per cent in 1961). The SPD – now an obedient Opposition within the context of the Restoration – obtained 39·3 per cent. The FDP, the party of the explicitly non-clerical section of the bourgeoisie and a small number of genuinely democratic intellectuals and petty-bourgeois (who, however, had no influence at all at this time) received 9·5 per cent (as opposed to 12·8 before). The only group in fundamental opposition, the German Peace Union (DFU), a pacifist-democratic party of intellectuals, won a mere 1·3 per cent. It was supported by the Communists, who had been illegal since 1956. The attempts of the Socialist Unity Party in the German

Democratic Republic to press for a formal discussion of fundamentals with all the West German parties, but essentially with the SPD (with parallel discussions between the trade unions of both countries), ended in failure after several incidents. The West German political criminal code still claimed validity for the area of the GDR, and therefore branded all the political representatives of the GDR as criminals. As late as 1966 it was only willing to permit an *ad hoc* law *ad personam* to halt prosecution by the Federal government for a limited period.

But the economic recession which began in 1966 soon threw the political fronts into disarray. The situation had already become less rigid at the first signs of the recession through a change in the political reaction of students and a very small number of progressive professors, who had previously been completely isolated in univerties which were essentially in the hands of lecturers taken over from the Third Reich and their students. The SPD had begun to criticize the small socialist student association, the SDS, in 1960, and expelled it from its ranks in 1961.

The SDS had become the core of a widespread student rebellion against the education system in the Federal Republic, against professors with a Nazi background, and then against support for reactionary regimes in the Third World (Persia) and against American policy in Vietnam. It also began to mobilize the public on the domestic political front. It campaigned against the long-standing attempts of Federal governments to 'supplement' the constitution of the Federal Republic with 'Emergency Laws', which were to confer dictatorial powers on the government in the case of a political crisis at home or abroad. In 1966 the Trade Union Congress resolved, by a large majority, to reject unconditionally any constitutional change of this kind, despite the energetic efforts of the leader of the Builders' Union and SPD Member of Parliament, Leber, to defend the emergency legislation. Soon after this, however, the party conference of the SPD declared, with only a few votes against, its willingness to cooperate in the legislation. The crucial factor was that the leader of the Metal Workers, Otto Brenner, at this time still supported the left-wing intellectual opposition. The leaders of the SPD also took part in a manoeuvre by the army, in which the 'emergency parliament' envisaged by the legislation – a conglomeration of a few 'higher' party leaders – was to be put to the test, although there was no legal basis for this.

The full outbreak of the economic recession led to the disintegration of the coalition government of the CDU/CSU and the FDP under the symbolic figure of the post-1948 capitalist 'economic miracle', Ludwig Erhard. To contain the crisis, the SPD offered itself as a coalition partner to the CDU, which had named the ex-Nazi Kiesinger as Federal Chancellor. In this government the SPD attempted to set in motion the long overdue adjustment of the Federal Republic's *Ostpolitik* to reality, but at the same time clung to its policy of not recognizing the GDR. Erhard's government had attempted to subject the trade unions to the decisions of government and management with the slogan of a 'planned society'; the SPD Minister of Economics, Karl Schiller (a professor of economics, who, like Kiesinger, had become a member of the Nazi party in the Third Reich), now sought to tame the wages policy of the unions and preserve them from any thoughts of workers' struggles with the slogan of 'concerted action'. The 'Grand Coalition' with Kurt Kiesinger as Chancellor and the SPD leader Willy Brandt as Deputy Chancellor and Foreign Minister, was formed on 1 December 1966. This government too retained the goal of changing the constitution through the emergency laws.

The result was a considerable growth in extraparliamentary activity by students on the one hand and by sections of the trade union officials on the other, who now openly attacked the SPD leadership. The Young Socialists, the organization for younger members of the SPD, came out in 1968 against the emergency legislation and in favour of the recognition of the GDR. Since then they have remained the backbone of an opposition within the SPD which is socialist in tendency, although it is continually weakened by disciplinary measures and party expulsions. They were not satisfied with the fact that diplomatic relations with Rumania were established with the declared reservation that the Federal government, regardless of Rumania's diplomatic relations with the GDR, still held to its claim to be the sole representative of Germany. It is well known that the GDR has never forced anyone to subscribe to a converse theory denying the existence of the Federal Republic.

Meanwhile the student rebellion continued. A student was shot dead by the police in a demonstration against the Shah of Persia's visit to the Senate of West Berlin. This led to solidarity demonstrations in all the universities, which became increasingly militant. They adopted increasingly revolutionary socialist slogans and proclaimed the rejection of the emergency laws as an immediate goal. In almost all the universities the leadership of student unions went over to the socialist students. After an attempt on 11 April 1968 to assassinate Rudi Dutschke (preceded by the incitement of the newspapers, especially those of the largest West German newspaper concern, the Springer Press), students and young workers in all the centres of the Federal Republic demonstrated against Springer's papers, invading their offices and burning their distribution vans. Several more demonstrators were killed by the police, and there were countless injuries and arrests. In conjunction with a few oppositional trade union leaders and many lower officials, especially in the chemical and metal workers' unions, the students organized a march on Bonn on 11 May 1968. This became a massive demonstration against the emergency laws. The leaders of the DGB, the national federation of all the trade unions, wanted to reduce the impact of this by organizing a parallel rally in Dortmund. A large number of participants, however, went from Dortmund to Bonn. Nonetheless, the government passed the emergency constitution with only minor modifications. The over-escalation of radical direct action tendencies, which followed this disappointment in the student movement and soon also destroyed the SDS, rapidly led to the disintegration of a nascent alliance between core groups in the working-class trade union movement and the intellectual opposition. The language gulf between workers and students tied to a specialized philosophical and sociological language always impeded this alliance in the past.

Nevertheless, the impact of the movement greatly altered the political situation in the Federal Republic. The attempt, at a conference in Offenbach in February 1968, to form a lasting political alliance between former Communists and non-SPD Socialists and the activists of this movement, failed because of these contradictions and particularly because of the Soviet occupation of Czechoslovakia.

But the Federal government did tolerate the new founding of a small legal Communist Party, the DKP, which was formed in September 1968 and had its founding party conference in April 1969. Admittedly, it has no influence as an electoral party, because the West German electoral system hinders the development of new (and small) parties. A large section of the workers do not want to lose the effect of their votes by giving them to a party which will not obtain any representation in parliament. Quite apart from this, the popularity of the DKP was immediately reduced by its clear support for the intervention of the Warsaw Pact states in Czechoslovakia. Following the decline of ultra-leftism in the student movement, however, the DKP, which offers students a realistic policy for the universities, gained control of important positions in the universities through its sympathizing student group 'Spartakus'. This, in turn, has an effect on young workers. The abstract, anti-bolshevik slogans of other parties and the professors have lost their former influence in the universities. The DKP, through emphasis on trade union demands and on the everyday interests of the workers, is trying gradually to increase its influence in the factories. It offers support and assistance to oppositional groupings in the SPD and the trade unions. Because of the nature of its social support the SPD must rely ultimately on the workers and white-collar workers. It is therefore possible that the SPD could, by external pressure, be forced again somewhat to the left as were the French Socialists after their profound moral collapse in the Algerian war.

There is a constant possibility of a new ban on the DKP and its student group, Spartakus (the KPD-ban of 1956, which has still not been repealed, could be applied to the DKP as a successor-organization). This is still advocated today, even by some administrative bodies headed by Social Democrats. In 1971, in a Federal state with a Social Democratic government, Bremen, approval was refused for the employment of a lecturer who had already been appointed, explicitly on the grounds of his DKP membership. This is a clear illustration of the limitations of this process at the present time.

The first consequence of the impulse from the student movement and the mass demonstrations against the emergency laws was that, even at the party conferences of the SPD, an end was put to the sepulchral peace which had characterized the Social Democrats since the Godesberg party conference in 1959. 'Left-wing' opponents dared to put forward political arguments at the Nürnberg party conference. This paved the way for an end to the coalition with the classical Restoration party, the CDU/CSU. The first move towards this was the election of the Social Democratic Gustav Heinemann as Federal President in opposition to the CDU candidate in 1969. Heinemann was also supported by the FDP, which was now really the opposition party to the Federal government. This tendency was greatly reinforced in September 1969, when, despite the upward trend of the economy, the Social Democratic Minister of Economics attempted to hold down workers' wage demands in the interests of the employers and 'stability'. His pressure on trade union leaders met with spontaneous resistance in the factories and there was a mass strike movement shortly before the Federal elections. It is true that the workers had undergone a process of depoliticization following their negative experiences in 1968, and they refused to have anything to do with political slogans. Many differences also remained between the indigenous workers and the almost two million South and South-East European workers employed in the Federal Republic. In many ways these prevented the formation of a clear class consciousness, especially since, in a recession like that of 1967–8, the immigrant workers are the first to lose their jobs and the German workers can regard their jobs as secure.

The spontaneous actions of the students, however, had taught the workers that, at least in everyday questions like wages, they could win concessions against the will of their trade union leaders who submitted to SPD and Government policies. They learned that trade union leaders could be forced into line by actions from below (the September strikes, 1969). It was this wave of strikes, and not the actions of the leaders of organized labour, which alone account for the substantial successes in wage demands which followed in the period of economic recovery in 1969 and 1970.

The federal elections in September 1969 increased the SPD vote to 42·7 per cent. The conservative party, the CDU/CSU, stagnated at 46·1 per cent, and the liberal bourgeois party, the FDP, came dangerously close to the 5 per cent clause of the electoral law by sinking to

5·8 per cent. The fascist NPD, which had registered substantial successes in all the regional elections during the recession, dropped below the 5 per cent limit again when faced with the renewed recovery of the economy. The SPD leaders now had the courage to form a government coalition with the FDP, which at least supported a (partial) relaxation of Cold War foreign policy. This is what made the meetings, in Erfurt and Kassel, between Federal Chancellor Brandt and the President of the GDR, Willi Stoph, possible. The results so far include the Moscow Treaty with the USSR (12 August 1971) and the Warsaw Treaty with Poland (18 November 1970). Demands for the 're-establishment of the 1937 borders of the German Reich', made by previous West German Governments and by the SPD itself after 1960, were thus abandoned and the existence of the second German state, the GDR, was accepted – albeit cautiously and inconsistently. It had become clear that the coalition of all the capitalist states, under the leadership of the USA, had become too weak to nullify the results of the Second World War by means of pressure or force. The SPD was thus forced to reconsider all its past efforts to adjust its ideas to the demands of the bourgeoisie, the CDU/CSU, and wide sections of the petit-bourgeoisie (especially refugees from the former German eastern regions and their representative organizations). It had to reverse its 1960 decision to adhere to the traditional *Deutschlandpolitik* of the Federal Republic.

In domestic affairs, the new government led by the SPD promised to bring the education system, at least to a limited extent, into line with elementary democratic requirements. This was because the achievements of the student movement had made the old system of university administration unworkable. It had also become generally known that the GDR's educational system, organized on the principle of ten years' general schooling, was far superior to that of the Federal Republic. The SPD's proposals were continually whittled down in compromises with the regional governments which, in this country with a strongly federal organization, were run by the CDU/CSU. There is now little hope of the SPD ever managing to implement in the whole of the Federal Republic the progressive measures which have already been introduced in several regions because of student pressure. The leaders of the Teachers' Union have already pointed out this contradiction several times.

In social and economic policy, too, little remains of the plans for reform. Inflationary tendencies in the Federal Republic have been somewhat weaker than in other capitalist states because of West Germany's strong economic position. The Social Democratic Minister of Economics and Finance, however, persists in his attempts to solve inflation and the dollar crisis at the expense of the workers and to the advantage of capital, and to impose his plans on the trade union leaders.

Despite its successes in foreign policy, therefore, this experiment of a predominantly Social Democrat government threatens to end in the same way as the experiment of the previous Wilson government in Great Britain, unless the unions can force it to change direction. It seems that the leaders of reformist labour parties in the various European states, having rejected their socialist goals in order to conform to monopoly capitalism, will only learn from their mistakes if they are forced to do so by the impulses of spontaneous mass movements or the pressure of stronger Marxist parties.

In France, the Chairman of the SFIO, Gaston Deferre, failed to persuade the SFIO party conference in 1965 to adopt a set of programmatic ideas which would sacrifice all socialist demands and put a stop to any efforts by SFIO members to cooperate with the PCF against the de Gaulle regime. Consequently, in the presidential election campaign of December 1965, François Mitterand, who then still represented a group of intellectuals and technocrats increasingly moving in the direction of socialist goals, rose to be the combined candidate of the entire Left, including the Communists. He won 32 per cent of the votes in the first round, and 45·5 per cent in the second. De Gaulle remained the winner with only 54·5 per cent. In the 1967 parliamentary elections, the SFIO put forward candidates only as part of a democratic Federation (in common with Mitterand's followers, but also with the Radicals, who supported the restoration of parliamentary democracy but not workers' demands and socialism). In the previous parliamentary elections, in 1962, the Radicals had received 7·7 per cent and the SFIO 12·6 per cent, but now the Federation could only muster 18·9 per cent. The PCF rose slightly from 22 per cent to 22·5 per cent; the PSU stagnated at 2·3 per cent. Nonetheless, a combination of the entire Left was formed for the second round, but it once again failed to prevent a Gaullist victory. The SFIO and the republican 'clubs' of the intelligentsia (as represented by Mitterand and others), became increasingly close, despite opposition to this policy by the right wing of the SFIO under Deferre. Together they were able to come to an agreement with the communists on an immediate 'platform'. This platform openly admitted their differences on a number of other questions.

The structural changes in French capitalism, due to the greater centralization of capital, as well as modernization and rationalization, had led to an increase in the role of the technical 'cadre'. In a state which still possessed, in the PCF, a strong workers' party with political class consciousness, a large number of these 'cadres' were brought into proximity with socialist ideas. Moreover, in France – in contrast to West Germany – the CGT and the CFDT were quite prepared to use the strike weapon and to call one-day general strikes.

The Gaullist regime, directed by representatives of the management of the largest concerns, aimed to overcome the crisis of the antiquated French education system (characterized by an excessive emphasis on achievement at school and university), by 'rationalizing' the period of study for future teachers. 'General studies', which preserved critical scientific analysis, were to be eliminated in favour of narrower, specialized study. Student resistance to these plans, however, soon coincided with the radicalization of the working masses, whose living standards had been reduced by rises in prices without parallel wage increases. The students had already started to fight against these government measures in the autumn of 1967. From February 1968, beginning in the crucial university of Nanterre, they had gone over to more forceful demonstrations. In the first days of May they came into increasingly bitter conflict with the police. This happened even more when the students adopted the tactic of occupying university buildings. On 10 May 1968 the police committed new, serious and bloody excesses against the students. Spontaneous mass strikes followed, which were, however, immediately taken over by the CGT and the CFDT (naturally supported by the PCF and the PSU). The general strike proclaimed by the trade unions – envisaged by the leaders as a limited protest strike against the police and for concrete material demands of workers – gripped not only Paris, but the whole of France. It involved spontaneous actions by workers, 'cadres' and students. By demanding the take-over of factories by the workers and actually occupying them, the problem of the struggle for power was posed in a practical way, because the positions won in many places could not be held without the winning of political power. In parliament, however, the Left was unable to bring down the Cabinet. The leaders of the PCF argued that prospects for an armed struggle for power were hopeless because the army, particularly the tank forces which were mostly made up of professional soldiers, stood firmly behind de Gaulle and the Government. Without exploring other types of challenge to the bourgeois regime the PCF and the CGT pressed the masses taking part in the actions to limit their demands and to agree to a com-promising retreat. On the other hand the Trotskyist, Maoist and Syndicalist groups who had sparked off the action of the masses, as well as the PSU, which was influential among intellectuals, con-sidered it unnecessary to retreat. They argued that the workers' leaders should never have helped the bourgeoisie to reconstitute its regime and should have had more confidence in the collective power of the workers to prevent any attempt to repress them forcibly. Instead de Gaulle and the government came out the winners although they had to grant a number of reforms and concessions and an amnesty for participants in the struggles of May and June. This defeat temporarily destroyed the united front of the Left and rein-forced the Right for a considerable period, leading to inevitable discussions within the working-class movement. The parliamentary elections at the end of June 1968 were the instrument and expression of bourgeois recovery: in the first round the Federation dropped to 16·5 per cent and the PCF to 20 per cent of the votes: only the PSU – as the seemingly most radical party – improved its position to 4 per cent. But the bourgeois regime had been badly shaken. This was revealed once more when de Gaulle failed in the Plebiscite of April 1969 to achieve a change of constitution by referendum. His aim had been to outmanoeuvre the working-class movement in particu-lar, but also the non-Gaullist section of the bourgeoisie, who advocated a change in foreign policy to pro-Americanism and friendlier relations with the EEC. Following de Gaulle's resignation, the PCF (despite the negative effects of the Czech crisis on its prestige) rose above 21 per cent once more in the first round of the presidential elections in June 1969, while the PSU was able to maintain its position and the Trotskyist candidate received 1 per cent. Deferre again became the SFIO candidate because of the contradictions arising from discussion on the defeat in May 1968 and the anticommunist atmosphere which followed the Czech crisis. But he only attracted 5 per cent of the voters, i.e. only the loyal organizational core whose support of the reformist party was unconditional. This failure of the SFIO, however, was the beginning of a turn to the left and the re-establishment of an alliance with the PCF. Further discussions within the SFIO and between the SFIO and the socialist clubs resulted in their amalgamation in 1971 in the new French Socialist Party (PSF). Mitterand, an advocate of a united front with the Communists, was now at its head. The PCF has continued to support the principle of a united front with all working-class parties, for a broad struggle against the presidential regime and the domination of capital.

At the PCF party conference in 1970 the most radical critics of the Soviet intervention in Czechoslovakia were condemned and the way paved for the expulsion of their spokesman, the philosopher Roger Garaudy. However, cooperation by the large working-class parties in the parliamentary and extraparliamentary fields, and cooperation between the trade unions of the CGT and the CFDT, and sometimes also the right-wing Force Ouvrière, is guaranteed for the present. It is also strong enough, despite the formally and judicially reactionary system of French constitutional law (compared, for example, to that of West Germany), to protect the legality of workers' actions, which is more than is possible in West Germany, where anti-Communist hysteria prevails and the SPD has ceased to think in terms of class struggle.

As the events of 1968 proved, the basic aim of the main forces in the French working-class movement remains the legal conquest of political power and the defence of bourgeois democratic laws. The PCF and CGT (but also the majority of the CFDT and a minority of the Socialist Party), assert that participation in elections and parliamentary disputes should reflect the struggles of the working population and its allies outside parliament, in demonstrations and strikes.

On the other hand, the May Events increased the influence of those forces among students, young workers, and the Marxist intelligentsia who regard the thesis of a 'legal' road to socialism as an illusion. They insist that the working class can only take power through workers' councils (soviets) and armed struggle. This struggle must be revolutionary in form as well as in content. Bourgeois-democratic legality cannot be the instrument of its own supersession, it must be exploded by popular force. These militants are gathered around two Trotskyist and two Maoist circles, but also have influence in the PSU. However their influence is still relatively small in times of social peace.

The workers' movement in Italy faced similar problems in its development, although in less dramatically accentuated forms. The Socialists first became fully aware of the period of stability in Italy when, after the Hungarian uprising in 1956, Nenni and the PSI withdrew from the united front they had until then had with the Communists. They soon turned to a coalition of the 'left centre' with the Christian Democrats. The amalgamation of the PSI and the right-wing PSDI as the PSU at the end of October 1966 was only the logical consequence of this change. But the contradictions remained. A large number of socialist officials stayed in the CGIL, a joint organization with the Communists, although the former leaders of the right-wing Social Democrats (PSDI) called on them to withdraw. In local politics, too, the majority of the old PSI members wanted to continue cooperation with the Communists. The class struggle assumed increasingly bitter forms in the second half of the sixties following the end of the period of stability and consolidation. The contradictions in the Socialist Party (which reassumed the name PSI in October 1968) quickly became more acute. This was encouraged by the Communists, who had long pursued a skilful and successful policy of a united front with left-wing Catholics in the working class. The Catholic Workers' Associations were forced to cooperate with the CGIL, whose authority increased accordingly.

The parliamentary elections in May 1968 were an unmistakable expression of the sharpening of class antagonisms. Such antagonisms are constantly reproduced structurally – even without crisis fluctuations – by the increasing depression of the industrially undeveloped South and the constant emigration of workers to the industrially highly developed North and to West Germany. The PSU, as it was then called, only received 14·5 per cent of the votes. In 1963 the PSI had still managed to poll 13·8 per cent and the PSDI 6·1 per cent, i.e. almost 20 per cent together. In contrast, the left-wing Socialists (PSIUP) won 4·5 per cent and the PCI rose from 25·3 per cent to 26·9 per cent. This clear defeat for the PSU (which was soon to be renamed the PSI) inevitably heightened the contradictions among its ranks. The extreme anti-communist wing, the earlier PSDI, no longer stood any chance of implementing its thesis of a complete ban on local and trade union cooperation with Communists, although Nenni came to their aid with a compromise resolution at a Party Central Committee meeting in July 1969. Nenni had to resign as Party leader and the anti-communist wing was forced to reconstitute itself as a separate party. This party split led, like the 1968 elections, to a temporary crisis in the 'left-centre' coalition, which seeks to preserve the balance of the capitalist power system by marginal concessions to the working class.

There have been repeated waves of demonstrations and strikes, organized jointly by the CGIL and the Catholic Associations, but also supported by the members of the weak Social Democratic Unions. The continual increase in the power of the CGIL has only occasionally suffered setbacks. This is due to the skilful policy of the PCI, which has been led by Longo and Berlinguer since Togliatti's death. Its strategic goal is to replace the 'left-centre' coalition by an alliance of the socialist parties and left-wing Catholics, which would carry out a policy of reforms structurally altering the relations of production after obtaining power by legal means. The Communists avoided (or absorbed) negative side-effects of the Czech crisis by issuing an unequivocal condemnation of the Soviet intervention. They openly discussed the question with a representative of the Soviet Politbureau at their Party Conference in February 1969. There is as much room for free expression in the Party as there was in most Communist Parties in the pre-Stalinist period of the Third International. The PCI's strategy has improved the chances of an amalgamation of the CGIL and the Catholic Workers' Associations, and the preparatory agreements for this have already been reached.

The PCI's strategy of employing the legality of parliamentary democracy at a time of extraparliamentary class struggles has given a temporary boost to groups which condemn this policy as 'revisionist'. This is especially the case among militant sections of the students and the intelligentsia, but also among younger workers. A group around the magazine *Manifesto* has been forced out of the PCI and a number of other revolutionary groups exist. The Syndicalist movement has also revived, although only among small groups. Despite their growing significance the groups of the far left have not at all displaced the PCI as the mass party of Italian workers. In this, too, Italian left-wing politics follow the French pattern.

Even this brief survey of the European working-class movement and its organizations in the capitalist states in the past half decade suggests how strongly they are influenced by developments in the socialist countries of Europe. The current standard of living of the working class, which is much higher than in earlier periods, could not have been attained in any of the European countries without the rival existence of the socialist states. After the Second World War the capitalist classses were convinced that the only way to regain the loyalty of the working classes and prevent them from being influenced by the politics of socialist countries was to grant them concessions. This also accounts for the extent of democratic rights still enjoyed by the working-class movement in many countries. The October Revolution and the other Socialist revolutions which arose in the wake of the Second World War thus remain a vital factor in the struggle of the working class, although this is seldom realized by the reformists.

Despite successes in some fields, the socialist countries continue to lag behind the industrially developed nations of Western Europe and the USA in the development of productivity. They are forced to set aside large sums of money for armaments because of their objectively antagonistic relation to the capitalist states. The transition to communism in the socialist states is still no more than a remote objective.

This constantly gives rise to new contradictions in their economic, social and political development, which often in their turn hinder the development of European working-class parties and trade unions in the 'West'. The problem becomes particularly clear when these contradictions reach dramatic proportions: the period of Stalinist terror in the USSR before the Second World War, or the period of neo-Stalinist terror and the split between the USSR and Yugoslavia in the initial phase of the Cold War, the events of 17 June 1953 in the GDR, the revolts in Poland and above all in Hungary in 1956, the Czechoslovakian crisis in 1968 and the Sino-Soviet split. The Polish crisis in December 1970 did not have the same negative effects on the Western European working-class movement because it was quickly absorbed internally.

The basic problems of the USSR and the CPSU are much the same as in 1965. The harsh effects of remnants of a Stalinist mentality on the life of society are undiminished. The ensuing limitations on freedom of discussion, however, have not prevented the emergence of oppositional currents, despite the danger of 'deviations' from current official attitudes being taken as signs of mental illness.

The emergence of Soviet policies which diverge from those of the second socialist world power, the People's Republic of China, was almost inevitable in view of their different historical origins. These differences took on dangerous forms with the Ussuri border conflict in 1969. Factional dogmatism and mutual accusations of heresy have now become familiar within the international Communist movement – a situation comparable to the conflict between the Soviet Union and Yugoslav Communists after 1948. Even the wisdom of Ho Chi Minh's call for the re-establishment of unity within the international Communist movement, contained in the political testament published after his death on 3 September 1969, has done nothing to soften the lines in this conflict. The Czech crisis and the conflict over Rumanian foreign policy serve as a reminder that for both Russia and China there is a danger of objective necessities of national defence being elevated into a permanent abstract right of great-power intervention. The self-preservation instinct of bureaucratic and hierarchical party structures makes this danger all the more real.

The prevention of nuclear conflicts and the negotiation of agreements to limit arms continue to be a clear and central aim of Soviet foreign policy, not least so that economic resources can be redirected to the immediate needs of the population and greater emphasis can be given to the production of consumer goods. The Soviet Union has been successful in creating, at the cost of great economic sacrifices, a relative military balance with the strongest capitalist world power, the USA. The first steps have been taken towards a change in the content and methods of economic planning. More consumer goods are being produced and there has been a limited relaxation of centralized planning. A start was made in the price reform of 1970, and this was endorsed and developed by the 24th Party Congress of the CPSU.

The greatest blow to any socialist state and its leading party during this period, and consequently also to the authority of the CPSU in the European working-class movement, occurred in Czechoslovakia. The beginnings of de-Stalinization under Novotny produced a degree of 'liberalization' both in society and in the Party. The real nature of the post-war trials of the Party leadership began to be publicly investigated. There were no fundamental changes, however. A number of critical reactions inside the Writers' Association in June 1967, and student demonstrations in October of the same year, led to a swing in the Party which was to alter the situation. In January 1968 Dubček replaced Novotny as First Secretary of the Party. While the intellectuals continued to play the leading role, wider groups (not only within the Party) began to join in the process of political discussion. The process was spontaneous, because basically the Party merely reflected the revulsion against Stalinism in the rest of society. To begin with it was not in a position to perform anything more than a limited role of its own. Most of the intellectuals who took part, and who were supported and followed by a large number of the new Party leaders, aimed at establishing a framework of genuinely socialist goals. They merely demanded democratic rights and humanitarian forms of socialism, as in the two-thousand-word Manifesto, which came to be regarded by many as a programme. The removal of strict control by the state and Party also led to the clear emergence of anti-Communist and anti-Soviet moods, however, especially among the the middle classes and the expropriated upper classes of former times. A group of old Party officials who had been close to Novotny sought to claim that these groups had the potential to become a pro-'Western' counter-revolutionary force, aiming to restore capitalism, if the Party did not abandon its passive stance. The fears they sought to arouse were fed not only by the proximity of West Germany but also by the theory of a 'socialist market economy' developed by Professor Sik, a member of the new Party leadership. The liberal danger to the Party's political monopoly seemed even greater because the Party was simultaneously being weakened by the reorganization of the Republic as a federation of nationalities. It was at this stage that the other states of the Warsaw Pact, with the exception of Rumania, started to intervene in the process under the leadership of the USSR. Constant negotiations and conferences took place, initially with the participation of the new Czech Party leaders. It was impossible to find a solution, however, which would preserve the credibility of both sides. By the Spring of 1968 Dubček and the new leadership announced a thoroughgoing reform of the old bureaucratic methods in their Action Programme and went ahead with plans for convening an extraordinary Congress of their Party which would consolidate the new course. Alarmed by these developments the USSR, whose policy was determined by the collective leadership of Brezhnev as First Secretary of the CPSU, Kosygin as Prime Minister and Podgorny as Chairman of the Presidium of the Supreme Soviet, decided to send in its troops. The other satellite states of the Warsaw Pact gave their support. Rumania was the only one which refused to take part. The invasion was carried out on 20 and 21 August 1968. Czechoslovak troops offered no resistance. A request for intervention by an old Stalinist group within the Party was quoted as justification by the occupying troops. Widespread passive resistance to the occupation led to dramatic negotiations with the leaders of the Czechoslovakian Party and Government in Moscow. The Czechoslovaks were made to accept Brezhnev's *ad hoc* thesis of the limited sovereignty of socialist states, which are not allowed to reverse, by their own decision, the development towards socialism (and that – at least in practice – the USSR was the sole judge of when this development was endangered). This, at least, was the official justification given out in the West. Consequently, the decisions of the Secret Conference of the Czech Party which met in a workers' district of Prague during the first days of the occupation were regarded as illegitimate and null.

The heated conflict over the intervention helped to halt the élan of socialist advances in France and West Germany in 1968. The smaller Communist Parties in Western Europe (e.g. the illegal German KPD: the new German Communist Party (DKP) had not yet been formed but later adopted the same position) were the only ones who gave unconditional support to the Soviet action. The only large party which has insisted on its opposition has been the Italian one. For a long time afterwards, the Czechoslovakian people, including the working class, persisted in bitter condemnation of the intervention. The demonstrations following a Czech–Soviet ice-hockey match in March 1969 showed the continuing strength of popular feeling. Resignation and passive acceptance followed. After a fluctuating period, the Party was successfully 'normalized' and adjusted to the occupation under the leadership of Gustav Husak.

No new major crisis has interrupted the direction which Hungary and its Socialist Workers' Party began to take soon after the group around Kadar re-established stable leadership. Despite the crisis in Czechoslovakia, and Hungary's participation in the intervention, the same tendencies towards a certain liberalization have continued to develop. Confirmation of this is the fact that the great Hungarian Marxist theorist, Georg Lukács, who died in 1971, was readmitted to the party despite his involvement in the events of 1956 and his differences with the USSR. The system of planning has been largely freed from bureaucratic obstructions since 1968, and a 'new economic mechanism' with a 'flexible price system' was endorsed by the Party Conference in November 1970. The developments of the next few years will show how far this approximation to the conceptions of Sik will go. In Bulgaria the situation remains much as it was in the early sixties. There have been no basic shifts, if one disregards small correctives in the mechanisms of planning and a slight liberalization of discussion in cultural questions.

The Socialist Unity Party (SED) and governing system of the German Democratic Republic have had a chance to test fully their new planning system which has led to substantial economic progress. This was only made possible by the construction of the Berlin Wall in 1961, which put a stop to the emigration of qualified workers into the Federal Republic. This drain had inflicted great economic losses on the GDR, which had borne the high costs of their training. In recent years, the new planning system has revealed its limitations on many questions. It has been supplemented by new experiments aimed at extending the production of consumer goods and the intensification and exploitation of modern methods of production. Official theorists have also begun to question the theory of socialism as an 'independent system', historically placed between capitalist relations of production and the goal of a communist society. In recent years, they claim, this had become too dogmatic, and served as a conceptual model too close to the structuralist system-theories of many contemporary non-Marxist political scientists in the capitalist countries. It is now being exposed to discussion and criticism, so that, within certain limits, theoretical discussion is taking place within the Party. The SED can afford to tolerate this slight relaxation of its former strictness since the GDR is currently undoubtedly the most industrialized and modernized country in Comecon. The bourgeois states, and in particular, West Germany, can no longer hope to liquidate the GDR by means of 're-unification', and the GDR's recognition in international law, even by the bourgeois states, cannot be far away after the Moscow Treaty and Four Power Agreement on West Berlin in 1971. However the siege mentality and situation remain, strengthening the position of the leading group in the SED and lessening the possibility of a move towards real workers' democracy in the GDR.

The Party structure in Poland was relaxed when Gomulka became leader after the conflicts of 1956, but harsh control was reimposed within the Party in the ensuing years, in spite of some industrial successes. The predominance of individual small peasants in the structure of agricultural production, with only small steps towards collectivization, strengthens the position of the Catholic higher clergy *vis-à-vis* the Party. In order to overcome this limitation on its rule in domestic affairs, the Party decided not only to come to a compromise, but also to impose stricter internal discipline and limit the freedom of public debates. The leaders of theoretical and philosophical debates in the working-class movement (e.g. Leszek Kolakowski, who was forced out of the Party after the Czech crisis and went into emigration, and Adam Schaff), suffered a visible reduction in their opportunities for expression and influence. The appearance of new contradictions in the economic structure in the mid-sixties was accompanied by expressions of sympathy for Israel in the 1967 Middle East conflict by small groups among the minority of Jews in Poland who had not been murdered in the Third Reich. Because of the anti-imperialist and therefore pro-Palestinian policy of the socialist countries, this sparked off an anti-Zionist campaign within the Party. In many cases it was exploited by the traditionally anti-semitic Catholic church. Support from some opportunist groups in the Party produced a shameful campaign which drove a section of the Jewish population into emigration. As a result of the developments in Czechoslovakia, an opposition movement began among students and writers, but it was quickly and successfully absorbed. The reaction of the Party leadership, however, was to reimpose strict limits on discussion within the Party. Concessions by the Party leaders to small peasant producers led to a heavy rise in food prices at the end of 1969. The workers, especially in the large coastal towns of the North, responded with a mass strike movement, and the government, on the advice of the Party leadership under Gomulka, sent in troops. The spread of the strike movement led to clashes in which demonstrators were shot. A crisis developed within the Party, and Gomulka was relieved of his post. The leadership was taken over by Gierek, who formerly led the Party organization in Upper Silesia, and who was more in touch with the working class. A compromise solution ended the strike without any further crisis in the political system and without negative effects in the West.

The situation of the workers' party in Rumania, which has been led by Ceaucescu since the death of Gheorghiu-Dej in 1965, continued to be characterized by its efforts for greater independence in foreign policy (and in international Communist affairs) from the USSR, while maintaining the old party structure internally. This was shown in the maintenance and extension of their relations with the Chinese Communists and in their opposition to any tendencies towards centralization in the Council for Mutual Economic Assistance (Comecon) and the Warsaw Pact. In 1968, they refused support for the intervention in Czechoslovakia. They condemned the invasion, and from the beginning of 1969 they have constantly and systematically improved their relations with Yugoslavia, not least because China at this time adopted a similar course. In relations with capitalist states, too, the Rumanians did not feel bound by the tactical conceptions of the other Warsaw Pact states, as was shown by the establishment of diplomatic relations with West Germany and President Nixon's visit to Rumania in 1969. Nonetheless, they consciously avoided a break with Soviet foreign policy, and concluded a Friendship Treaty with the USSR in 1970. Economic construction was accelerated by investments from capitalist countries, without endangering the system of centralized planning. Internationally, the Rumanian Communists are consciously prepared to risk limited conflicts with the other European socialist countries, especially the USSR, and this policy has been endorsed by Party Conferences in 1969 and 1971.

The Communists in Albania have maintained their close relationship with the Chinese Communist Party, not only during the Cultural Revolution, when Party structures dissolved in the spontaneous mass movement of the Chinese Red Guards, but also in the period of reconstruction and centralized consolidation of party structures in China. They have also given their full approval to China's new involvement in power politics, and to its course of obtaining influence by means of alliances which seem opportune at the time. This was revealed as early as April, 1969, when the Central Committee of the Albanian Communist Party issued a declaration calling for closer cooperation with Yugoslavia and Rumania. Although Albania was very backward before 1945, substantial assistance from the Chinese has furthered the process of internal industrialization, so that today it is economically more advanced than the Albanian parts of Yugoslavia.

The Federation of Communists in Yugoslavia has continued to suffer from strong tensions because of the inequality of industrial development in the various republics of a country organized along federal lines. This inequality was reinforced by the excessive federalization of economic planning and by the 'socialist market economy', which, in addition, makes it more difficult to exercise full control over investments from capitalist countries. On the one hand, these tensions result in repeated conflicts between the party organizations in the member republics and the influence of the central leadership; on the other, they encourage attempts by sections of the intelligentsia to implement a revisionist adjustment to ideologies current in the capitalist countries. A rapprochement with the USSR, which had been developing for some years, was interrupted once more by the invasion of Czechoslovakia. Meanwhile relations with China have greatly improved.

There has been little progress towards greater working-class unity at an international level. The reformist labour parties of Western Europe continue to comprise the great majority of the Socialist International. Even at its Congress in Helsinki in 1971, this body did not abandon its Cold War positions and its ban on cooperation with communist parties. This Conference showed once again however that the Socialist International is incapable of promoting cooperation even among its own member parties. In practice it provides little more than the opportunity for the loose exchange of views between the leaders of the individual parties, and of these the Finnish, Italian and French socialists have long ceased to respect the ban on relations with the Communists. The International Federation of Free Trade Unions (ICFTU), despite its dubious antecedents is of more significance since it performs immediately practical tasks in the field of international trade union cooperation. It coordinates trade union policy for the International Labour Office, for other agencies of the UN and for the institutions of the EEC. After the extreme advocate of anti-communism, the AFL/CIO of the USA, withdrew, the Federation largely abandoned its anti-communism, although this is unfortunately not yet the case in its policy towards the under-developed countries of Africa and Asia. The World Federation of Trade Unions (WFTU) continues to embrace the trade unions of the socialist states (the Yugoslavs, however, only participate as 'obser-vers'), but it also includes the associations of many non-European countries, as well as the CGIL in Italy and the CGT in France, i.e. the strongest trade union centres in these countries. The Communist Parties have had no permanent international organization since the dissolution of the Communist International in 1943 and the Cominform in 1956. Their International Conferences, however, often have definite significance for the practical behaviour of the parties which take part. The European parties (except at their own special conferences) have long ceased to be predominant, and a large number of parties from other continents stand at their side. Because of the split between the Soviet and Chinese camps, parties close to the Chinese position, and also a group of Asian parties who refuse to join either camp, have boycotted these conferences. The Chilean party, however, continues to participate: in alliance with the Socialist Party of Allende (who was once a Trotskyist) and left-wing Catholic and radical groups, it is beginning to take the road which the 1957 Conference of Communist Parties recommended for those countries where it was feasible: viz. the conquest of political power by defending and exploiting the democratic possibilities of the still bourgeois state, in order to initiate socialist reorganization of the economy and society. This strategy has become a model for most of the European Communist parties in capitalist states and already determines the policy of the PCF and the PCI, the two largest West European Parties. Despite their criticism of the Soviet intervention in Czechoslovakia, they still participate regularly in the discussions at the International Conferences of Communist Parties. Meanwhile the Trotskyist Fourth International, which rejects the parliamentary road to socialism, now has small groups in most European countries though they also are prone to splits and divisions.

There have been great national variations in the development of the workers' movement in the different European countries during this period. But the above survey again underlines the fact that the prospects of the workers in the different zones of Europe are closely intertwined: an advance or a setback for the workers in one country tends to be an advance or a setback for the workers' movement throughout the continent. In particular the fate of the workers' struggles in the capitalist West is strongly interconnected with the fate of socialism in the East. To begin with, the mere existence of a non-capitalist zone in Europe is a factor of crucial significance for the class struggles in the capitalist countries. It induces caution in the ruling class of the capitalist half of Europe and sets certain limits on their prosecution of the class war. The working-class parties in the West have a direct interest, even from the point of view of the reformist wing, in the continued existence of the socialist states in the world; anything that weakens these states also gravely weakens the position of the workers inside every capitalist country.

On the other hand contradictions and reversals in the transition to socialism in the East lead to negative consequences for the working-class movement in the capitalist states. This was clear at the time of the profound crisis in the USSR and CPSU during the Great Depression and the subsequent victorious advance of fascism in the capitalist countries. Since the Second World War the suppression of the Hungarian uprising in 1956 and the intervention in Czechoslovakia in 1968 prove that setbacks in the East have immediate repercussions in the West. In general all neo-Stalinist distortions produce victories for Cold War ideology in the workers' movement in the capitalist states. These are all the greater if Communist Parties see their role as that of justifying the actions of the existing regimes in the East. This only increases still further the influence of the social democratic parties among the working masses. The process of transforming backward capitalist societies into developed socialist societies is bound to be long and difficult: it cannot be accomplished at one stroke but requires continual new struggles. It will be necessary for the workers progressively to make their own the states which have been established in their name but which they are as yet too weak really to control. Despite periods of stagnation and regression the appearance of a movement of renewal in each new generation in the socialist states is proof that the struggle will continue until it establishes fully democratic workers' power. It is still essential to remember that all socialist revolutions so far have suffered from the initial disadvantage that the capitalist economic order continues to prevail in those countries where the forces of production are most highly developed after centuries of capitalist and imperialist accumulation. The struggle for socialism has had to contend with the enormous military and economic strength of the capitalist powers. Moreover the problems of the socialist states still engaged in primitive capital accumulation have been greatly aggravated by internal contradictions and distortions. Bureaucracy and ideological rigidity have repeatedly flourished in the isolation and scarcity to which these early socialist regimes have been subject. In the extreme case this could lead, through capitulation to the predominant position of the capitalist world, to the open abandonment of socialism. In the past, particular reformist parties such as the West German SPD have abandoned socialist objectives under capitalist pressure. But the character of a socialist state is less variable than that of a socialist party operating within a bourgeois political context – the nationalization of the basic means of production and the overthrow of the political power of the former possessing classes create objective barriers to the re-emergence of capitalist social relations even where socialism has ceased to be the subjective commitment of the leading group. That is why up to now capitalism has not been restored in those lands where it has been overthrown despite many interruptions and regressions in the task of building socialism. The first socialist revolutions are no doubt as distant from full communism (a classless world society which can fully develop labour and every other human potentiality) as the early bourgeois revolutions of the seventeenth and eighteenth century were distant from modern fully developed capitalism. The uneven development of socialist revolution internationally creates the possibility of tension between the various socialist states with a consequent dogmatization and mutual provocation which obscures the need for international solidarity against imperialism. However there is reason to believe that the present discrepancies between China and the Soviet Union are likely to be no more permanent than those which in the past separated the Soviet Union and Yugoslavia. But meanwhile those who pay the price of these antagonisms are those in the front lines of the struggle against imperialism.

The main advance of socialism in this period has been the successes of the national liberation movements, especially in South East Asia, in combating the military might of US imperialism. This has been an inspiration to revolutionaries everywhere. At the same time the growing internal crisis in the capitalist world opens up the possibility for a renewal of the working-class movement in the homelands of imperialism. The signs of this malaise now appear unmistakably in the growing international rivalry of the imperialist states in the aftermath of the international financial crisis of August 1971, and in the generalized tendency for productive forces to stagnate, for price inflation to continue and for large-scale unemployment to reappear in most major capitalist states. We have seen above how the 1966–7 recession in Europe produced a significant rise in the economic militancy of workers in most European countries and at least one major political explosion: the May events in France. However, as we have also seen, the predominant pattern of political organization was relatively unchanged by these developments. As the economic troubles of the European capitalist states grow, the necessity for a more adequate political response within the workers' movement should be more widely recognized. Even in the United States there are signs of a new spirit of struggle in the workers' organizations, despite the heavy legacy of imperialist corruption of the trade unions and the pervasive influence of Cold War ideology. In Europe the prospect of a heightened class struggle can only mean that the workers will either allow themselves to become the victims of a new period of capitalist readjustment or that they will again rediscover the historic mission of their class: the sounding of a revolutionary tocsin which will summon all the oppressed and the exploited to overthrow the regime of capitalist private property in Europe, the continent that gave it birth.

November 1971

Further Reading

Publishers' note : This list has been adapted and lengthened for the English-language edition with the aim of enabling the English-speaking reader to follow up in more depth the chief topics of the book. Limitation to works written in or translated into English necessarily involves leaving some gaps, but an attempt has been made to cover the main subjects and events. Whenever possible references have been given to the edition of a work most readily available.

GENERAL WORKS

Beer, Max, *The General History of Socialism and Social Struggles*, New York, 1957.

Cole, G. D. H., *A History of Socialist Thought*, 5 vols, London, 1953–60.

Dobb, Maurice, *Studies in the Development of Capitalism*, London, 1963.

Hobsbawm, E. J., *The Age of Revolution, 1789–1848*, New York and London, 1962.

Landauer, Carl, *European Socialism*, 2 vols, Berkeley and Los Angeles, 1959.

Lichtheim, George, *A Short History of Socialism*, London, 1970.

Lichtheim, George, *The Origins of Socialism*, London, 1969.

Mayer, Arno J., *The Politics and Diplomacy of Peacemaking : Containment and Counter-revolution at Versailles, 1919*, London, 1968.

Wilson, Edmund, *To the Finland Station*, London, 1960.

THE INTERNATIONALS

Borkenau, Frank, *The Communist International*, London, 1938.

Braunthal, Julius, *History of the International, 1864–1943*, 2 vols, London, 1966 and 1967.

Dutt, R. Palme, *The Internationale*, London, 1963.

Gruber, Helmut (ed.), *International Communism in the Age of Lenin. A Documentary History*, New York, 1967.

Haupt, Georges, *Socialism and the Great War : The Collapse of the Second International*, Oxford, 1972.

Joll, James, *The Second International, 1889–1914*, London, 1955.

THE WORKING-CLASS MOVEMENT IN INDIVIDUAL COUNTRIES

Britain and Ireland

Briggs, Asa (ed.), *Chartist Studies*, London, 1963.

Cole, G. D. H., *A Short History of the British Working-Class Movement, 1789–1947*, London, 1948.

Cole, G. D. H. and Postgate, Raymond, *The Common People, 1746–1946*, London, 1961.

Collins, Henry and Abramsky, Chimen, *Karl Marx and the British Labour Movement*, London, 1965.

Engels, Friedrich, *The Condition of the Working Class in England in 1844*, London, 1970.

Gallacher, William, *Revolt on the Clyde*, London, 1936.

Greaves, C. Desmond, *The Life and Times of James Connolly*, London, 1951.

Harrison, Royden, *Before the Socialists*, London, 1965.

Hobsbawm, E. J., *Labouring Men*, London, 1968.

Jackson, T. A., *Ireland Her Own*, London, 1970.

Kendall, Walter, *The Revolutionary Movement in Britain*, London, 1969.

MacFarlane, L. J., *The British Communist Party*, London, 1966.

Marx, Karl, *Capital*, vol. 1, New York and London, 1967.

Miliband, Ralph, *Parliamentary Socialism*, London, 1961.

Morton, A. L., *The Life and Ideas of Robert Owen*, London, 1969.

Pelling, Henry, *The Origins of the Labour Party, 1880–1900*, London, 1954.

Rudé, George and Hobsbawm, E. J., *Captain Swing*, London, 1970.

Semmel, Bernard, *Imperialism and Social Reform*, London, 1960.

Strauss, Erich, *Irish Nationalism and British Democracy*, London, 1951.

Thompson, Edward, *The Making of the English Working Class*, Harmondsworth, 1968.

France

Artz, F. B., *Reaction and Revolution, 1814–1832*, New York, 1934.

Bernstein, Samuel, *The Beginnings of Marxian Socialism in France*, New York, 1933.

Bernstein, Samuel, *August Blanqui and the Art of Insurrection*, London, 1971.

Blanc, Louis, *The History of Ten Years, 1830–1840*, 2 vols, London, 1844–5.

Brower, Daniel R., *The New Jacobins: the French Communist Party and the Popular Front*, New York, 1968.

Buonarrotti, Filippo, *History of Babeuf's Conspiracy for Equality*, London, 1836.

Duveau, Georges, *1848: The Making of a Revolution*, London, 1967.

Edwards, Stewart, *The Paris Commune*, London, 1971.

Goldberg, Harvey, *Jean Jaurès*, Madison, 1962.

Lefebvre, Georges, *The French Revolution*, 2 vols, London, 1962 and 1964.

Lissagaray, Prosper, *History of the Commune*, New York and London, 1971.

Manuel, Frank E., *The Prophets of Paris*, New York, 1965.

Marx, Karl, *The 18th Brumaire of Louis Napoleon*, Moscow and London, 1967.

Marx, Karl and Engels, Friedrich, *The Paris Commune*, London, 1971.

Ridley, F. H., *Revolutionary Syndicalism in France*, Cambridge, 1971.

Robertson, Priscilla, *Revolutions of 1848*, New York, 1960.

Singer, Daniel, *Prelude to Revolution. France in May 1968*, London, 1970.

Wohl, R., *French Communism in the Making, 1914-24*, Stanford, 1966.

Germany

Anderson, Evelyn, *Hammer or Anvil, the Story of the German Working Class*, London, 1945.

Bebel, August, *My Life*, London, 1912.

Engels, Friedrich, *Germany: Revolution and Counter Revolution*, London, 1969.

Frölich, P., *Rosa Luxemburg*, London, 1972.

Gay, Peter, *The Dilemma of Democratic Socialism. Eduard Bernstein's Challenge to Marx*, New York, 1962.

Hamerow, Theodore S., *Restoration, Revolution, Reaction: Economics and Politics in Germany, 1815-1871*, Princeton, 1966.

Luxemburg, Rosa, *Selected Political Writings*, New York, 1971.

Mayer, Gustav, *Friedrich Engels*, London, 1936.

Mehring, Franz, *Karl Marx, The Story of His Life*, London, 1951.

Morgan, R. P., *The German Social Democratic Party and the First International, 1864-1872*, Cambridge, 1965.

Nettl, J. P., *Rosa Luxemburg*, 2 vols, London, 1966.

Rosenberg, A., *The Birth of the German Republic, 1871-1918*, New York, 1964.

Ryder, A. J., *The German Revolution of 1918*, Cambridge, 1967.

Schorske, Carl F., *German Social Democracy, 1905-1917*, New York, 1965.

Russia

Balabanov, Angelica, *My Life as a Rebel*, London, 1938.

Baron, S. H., *Plekhanov; the Father of Russian Marxism*, London, 1963.

Carr, E. H., *A History of Soviet Russia (The Bolshevik Revolution, 1917-23*, 3 vols; *The Interregnum, 1923-4*, 1 vol; *Socialism in One Country, 1924-6*, 3 vols; *Foundations of a Planned Economy, 1926-1929*, 2 vols), London, 1950-72.

Deutscher, Isaac, *Trotsky: The Prophet Armed, 1879–1921*; *The Prophet Unarmed, 1921–1929*; *The Prophet Outcast, 1929–1940*, 3 vols, London, 1970.

Deutscher, Isaac, *Stalin*, Harmondsworth, 1966.

Deutscher, Isaac, *The Unfinished Revolution*, London, 1967.

Erlich, Alexander, *The Soviet Industrialization Debate, 1924–28*, Cambridge (Mass.), 1960.

Hill, Christopher, *Lenin and the Russian Revolution*, Harmondsworth, 1971.

Krupskaya, Nadezhda, *Memoirs of Lenin*, London, 1970.

Lane, David, *The Roots of Russian Communism*, Assen, 1969.

Lenin, Vladimir I., *State and Revolution*, Moscow and London, 1970.

Lewin, Moshe, *Lenin's Last Struggle*, London, 1970.

Liebman, Marcel, *The Russian Revolution*, London, 1968.

Nettl, J. P., *The Soviet Achievement*, London, 1967.

Reed, John, *Ten Days that Shook the World*, Harmondsworth, 1966.

Serge, Victor, *Memoirs of a Revolutionary, 1901–41*, London, 1967.

Sukhanov, N. N., *The Russian Revolution: a Personal Record*, London, 1959.

Trotsky, Leon, *The Revolution Betrayed*, New York, 1967.

Trotsky, Leon, *The Permanent Revolution*, New York, 1969.

Venturi, Franco, *Roots of Revolution*, London, 1962.

Eastern Europe

Bethell, Nicholas, *Gomulka. His Poland and his Communism*, London, 1969.

Blit, Lucjan, *The Origins of Polish Socialism*, Cambridge, 1971.

Davidson, Basil, *Partisan Picture*, Bedford, 1946.

Deakin, F. W. D., *The Embattled Mountain*, London, 1971.

Dedijer, V., *Tito Speaks*, London, 1953.

Dziewanowski, M. K., *The Communist Party of Poland*, Cambridge (Mass.), 1959.

Eudes, Dominique, *The Greek Partisans. Civil War in Greece, 1943–49*, London, 1972.

Fejtö, François, *History of People's Democracies*, London, 1971.

Hepple, Muriel and Singleton, Fred, *Yugoslavia*, London, 1961.

Ionescu, Ghita, *Communism in Rumania: 1944–1962*, London, 1964.

Jackson, George, *Comintern and Peasant in East Europe*, London, 1966.

Kovrig, Bennet, *The Hungarian People's Republic*, London, 1970.

Molnar, Miklos, *Hungary 1956*, London, 1971.

Pelikan, Jiri (ed.), *The Secret Vysoçany Congress of the Czech Communist Party*, London, 1971.

Rothschild, Josef, *The Communist Party of Bulgaria: Origins and Development, 1883–1936*, London, 1959.

Seton-Watson, Hugh, *The East European Revolution*, London, 1950.

Tökés, Rudolf, *Bela Kun and the Hungarian Soviet Republic*, New York and London, 1967.

Tsoucalas, Constantine, *The Greek Tragedy*, Harmondsworth, 1969.

Zinner, Paul E., *Communist Strategy and Tactics in Czechoslovakia, 1918–1948*, London, 1963.

Spain and Italy

Brenan, Gerald, *The Spanish Labyrinth*, Cambridge, 1950.

Cammett, John M., *Antonio Gramsci and the Origins of Italian Communism*, Stanford, 1969.

Delzell, Charles F., *Mussolini's Enemies: the Italian Anti-fascist Resistance*, Princeton, 1961.

Fiori, Giuseppe, *Antonio Gramsci: Life of a Revolutionary*, London, 1970.

Gramsci, Antonio, *Selections from the Prison Notebooks*, London, 1971.

Jackson, Gabriel, *The Spanish Republic and the Civil War, 1931–39*, Princeton, 1965.

Malefakis, Edward E., *Agrarian Reform and Peasant Revolution in Spain*, London, 1970.

Procacci, Giuliano, *History of the Italian People*, London, 1971.

Tarrow, Sidney G., *Peasant Communism in Southern Italy*, Yale, 1967.

Thomas, Hugh, *The Spanish Civil War*, Harmondsworth, 1968.

Scandinavia

Hodgson, J. H., *Communism in Finland*, Princeton, 1967.
Rustow, D. A., *The Politics of Compromise. Parties and Government in Sweden*, Princeton, 1955.

Modern Reader Paperbacks